Good Girl Work

GOOD GIRL WORK

FACTORIES, SWEATSHOPS, AND
HOW WOMEN CHANGED THEIR ROLE IN THE
AMERICAN WORKFORCE

Catherine Gourley

The Millbrook Press
Brookfield, Connecticut

Cover photograph courtesy of Corbis-Bettmann

Photographs courtesy of Stock Montage, Inc.: pp. 2-3, 8, 31, 90; Corbis-Bettmann: pp. 10, 12-13, 26, 28-29, 36, 40, 70; Culver Pictures, Inc.: pp. 14-15, 20, 38-39, 46, 86; The Granger Collection, New York: pp. 22-23, 62-63, 65; Corbis: p. 34; Pennsylvania State Archives: pp. 42-43; Chicago Historical Society: pp. 51 (The White Slave Girls of chicago by One of Them) (ICHi-29401), 76 (ICHi-21780); National Archives: p. 52, NWDNS-102-LH-245); North Wind Picture Archives: p. 56; Jacob A. Riis Collection, Museum of the City of New York (90.13.4.148): p. 60; UPI/Corbis-Bettmann: pp. 74-75, 92-93; The Schlesinger Library, Radcliffe College: p. 88

Library of Congress Cataloging-in-Publication Data
Gourley, Catherine.
Good girl work: factories, sweatshops, and how women changed their role in the American workforce / Catherine Gourley.
p.   cm.
Includes bibliographical references and index.
Summary: Discusses the girls and women in the industrial workforce of the nineteenth and early twentieth centuries, and the reforms and movements that changed their working conditions and the nature of the work iself.
ISBN 0-7613-0951-9 (lib. bdg.)
1. Children—Employment—United States—History—Juvenile literature.
2. Women—Employment—United States—History—Juvenile literature.
[1. Children—Employment. 2. Women—Employment.] I. Title
HD6250.U3G68   1999
331.3'1'0820973—dc21   98-35529   CIP   AC

Published by The Millbrook Press, Inc.
2 Old New Milford Road, Brookfield, Connecticut 06804

DEDICATION

In the 1950s when I was growing up in Wilkes-Barre, Pennsylvania,
the anthracite coal mining industry was waning. The silk and lace mills and
textile factories remained for a while longer and then they, too, began to shut
down and board their windows to be replaced in time by other industries.
Like Juanita Hinson, one of the girls featured in this book, I have always
been able to look beyond the culm banks and the brick factories to see great
beauty in Wyoming Valley and in the people of many nationalities, my own
Irish and German grandparents included, that were drawn to the valley by the
industry. They have worked very hard and honestly to make good lives for
themselves. In the summer of 1997, I returned home to Wilkes-Barre, after
many years living away, and wrote this book here where my roots are.
Although I never worked the long, tedious hours of the good girls in the
factories and mills and tenement sweatshops, I found I could relate to them
nevertheless, perhaps in part because I grew up here.

My appreciation goes to the librarians at Wilkes University who tracked down
some hard to get, out of print books by Nell Nelson, Agnes Nestor, and Mrs.
John and Maria Van Vorst; and to Dennis, who had saved from many years
ago his photocopy of Sarah Atherton's 1915 survey "The Wage Earning Girls
of Wilkes-Barre" which was the genesis of this book. Dennis believes very
strongly in the message of the book, that female child labor was worthy of its
own study, and so to him and to my hometown I dedicate *Good Girl Work*.

CONTENTS

Spinner in a Georgia cotton mill

INTRODUCTION

Small Girls Wanted

On an afternoon in 1897, Agnes Nestor stood in the manager's office of the Eisendrath Glove Factory in Chicago. She had come for a job, she said. The manager eyed her suspiciously. "How old are you?" he asked.

I was small for my age, Agnes remembered, *and wore my hair down my back in two long braids. When I said, "Fourteen," he snapped: "You look younger than that."*

Agnes's mother had come to the factory with her and now she spoke up. She assured the manager that her girl was old enough to work. Still, he turned Agnes away. Come back later, he advised the girl, then maybe he would consider her. Agnes was so filled with disappointment she could hardly speak.

Her defeat was short lived. Determined to help her family earn much-needed money, Agnes returned to the glove factory a few days later. This time the manager gave her a job operating a winding machine. Agnes would later write of her first day of work in the factory: *Around me in the small room, there was the clicking of the knitting machines, the humming of the sewing machines, but all this did not distract me. My own machine ran quietly and steadily. I concentrated on my work and was happy all day long.*[1]

In another city halfway across the country—Rochester, New York—two men were also looking for work. They stopped at the door of a large brick building. A sign posted there read: *Small Girls Wanted.* One man said to the other, "That's fourteen places we've seen they want kids today, Bill, but we've tramped round all week an' never got sight of a job."

Inside the brick building were rows and rows of sewing machines. Here, too, the air was full of constant clackering. Each machine was powered by steam and operated by girls. Many were fourteen or sixteen. Some were older; a few, younger. The smallest girls worked at making buttonholes or pulling threads from seams, the kind of work that little fingers can do quickly . . . and cheaply. Small hands did not cost as much as men's hands. And the hands of little girls were the cheapest labor of all.

In the late 1800s and early 1900s, thousands of women and children worked. They worked in large cities like Chicago, New York, Pittsburgh, and Rochester. They worked, too, in small mill villages in the mountains of Massachusetts, Pennsylvania, Tennessee, and North and South Carolina. They did more than wind thread and pedal sewing machines. They painted tins of canned meat. They sorted poultry feathers for hats. In laundries, they fed heavy wet clothes into mangle machines. In tenement buildings, they pasted hundreds of paper petals on stems to make artificial flowers.

In candy factories, as sheets of soft chocolate and maple caramels came from the oven and cooled, a dozen girls wrapped the square slices in paper and set them inside candy tins. Other girls stood at troughs filled with popcorn and gum-

Advertisement for Young & Smylie pure Calabria licorice lozenges, 1887

10

drops. All day they scooped the candy into paper bags and tied them off at the necks. Still others dipped sticks into steaming syrup pots, making stick candy. Wrapping and filling and dipping—this, too, was good girl work.

It was good for the owners of the factories and mills because employing girls meant greater profits. But the work was good for the girls, too—or so community leaders argued and many parents believed. The twelve hours each day the girls spent inside the factories kept them off the streets and out of trouble. And the two or three dollars they earned each week, though not very great, still helped to feed their hungry families.

Boys worked, too, of course. But girl work was different. The type of job given to a girl required little skill and provided little opportunity to learn a trade that could eventually bring her independence. Instead, the work usually involved repetitive, monotonous movements. Even when they performed the same jobs as boys, girls were paid less. They also managed their wages differently from boys. On pay day, good girls turned over their dollars to their mothers and fathers. Boys, especially as they matured into men, were more likely to keep the money for themselves.

Although the female workers had many different names—spinners, winders, and doffers; heelers, binders, and canners—they shared a common identification: They were all "girls," regardless of their age. It is what they called themselves and how society labeled them. Even when they grew up and became working wives and working mothers, they were still girls. Even when they grew old and the pace of their work slowed, they were "girls."

The good girls among them did not complain of the long hours, the low wages, or the poor lighting and bad air in the factories and mills. As long as Agnes Nestor reported to work on time and her fingers kept pace with the machines, she was a good girl. In time, though, Agnes began to resist the harsh factory rules that stiffened her mind as well as her body. She found it harder and harder to work happily all day long. One afternoon, she walked off her job and shouted at the other girls to walk out, too. They did.

In the early 1900s all across the country, thousands of working girls were joining together and marching through the streets with signs that de-

manded their rights as workers: higher wages, no speedups or slowdowns, a ten-hour day. Then the angry factory owners and the community leaders called them new names: rebels, traitors, criminals. They fired girls who dared to join a labor union. They hired thugs to harass and beat the girls who went on strike and paraded with pickets in the streets. The police arrested them, and the judges sentenced them to days and even weeks in prison. They weren't good girls anymore.

Like Agnes Nestor, many of the women who fought back against unfair and unsafe labor practices began working when they were children, some as young as nine and ten years old. In the letters, diaries, and poems they wrote, and in the personal reminiscences and interviews they gave labor reformers and newspaper reporters, comes the story of good girl work. It is the story of how working girls changed America forever.

Girls working in a Tampa, Florida, cigar box factory, 1909.

13

The first clatter of machinery is heard in a room . . . where "girls," who are always girls, no matter the age, sit with eyes and hands busy at sewing machines. No longer the "stitch, stitch, stitch" of the weary binder, but machines speeded at the rate of six hundred stitches in a minute!

Harpers' New Monthly Magazine,
January 1885

A Colonial New England woman spins, tends a child, and prepares food in this engraving. She most likely split the wood for the fire, as well.

CHAPTER ONE

The Coming of Machines

In America during colonial times, to be idle was to be a burden to society. Women were not idle. In the home, they tatted lace, carded wool, and spun flax into linen. They scoured the wooden tables and the plank floors and the pewter dishes. They tended gardens, and they nursed the sick. They didn't merely cook a meal. They fattened the poultry and smoked the ham. They boiled, fried, stewed, and fricasseed. Even gentry women—ladies of good birth and superior social standing in the community—were known to slaughter a cow. Some were trained by carving masters and could expertly "thigh a woodcock, wing a quail, mince a plover, or rear a goose." In the early 1700s, Colonel William Byrd of Virginia described his daughters' work in a letter to a friend in England. He wrote: "They are every Day up to their Elbows in Housewifery, which will qualify them effectually for useful Wives, and if they live long enough, for Notable Women."

A woman who worked was useful. A woman who worked was good.

Her labors were not limited to housewifery, however. In the community, women operated taverns, boardinghouses, and printing establishments. Some were milliners, sewing custom-made hats and gowns of the latest styles from England for ladies who could afford not to sew their own clothes. Others advertised their services in the local gazettes as menders of brocades and silks and china. Elizabeth Kelly of Annapolis, Maryland, advertised *her* services in repairing horse whips.

Deputy Husbands and Indentured Daughters

In December 1748, Mary Coates of Philadelphia placed an advertisement in the *Pennsylvania Gazette*. It read: " . . . sundry sorts of merchants goods . . . to be sold cheap, for ready money . . ." [2] Mary's husband Samuel had died, and her announcement told the community that the widow was assuming a new role: deputy husband. She had daughters and sons to support and she hoped to run her husband's business with the same reputation that he had enjoyed.

A woman who assumed her husband's business after his death, or in his absence due to any other reason, was sometimes called a "deputy husband." To be fair, a man who temporarily took on a woman's work could be called a "deputy wife," but that was rare. The fact remains that women's work in colonial times might have been useful and good, but women themselves had few rights, either as workers or wives. The common law of the times was this: Unmarried daughters were the property of their fathers. A single woman had rights of her own under the law, but once joined in wedlock to a husband, her will and her property became his, including any children they might have.

If he wished, a father could "put out" his children to work, selling their services as farmhands, chimney sweeps, maids, and cooks to other families or businesses. Colonial communities viewed such work as necessary in order to teach children—especially the children of poor families—self-dependence and thrift. A boy was likely to be put out as an apprentice, hired to a business for a period of years to learn a skilled trade. At the end of the contract, he earned his freedom and a place in the working community. A girl, however, was more likely to be put out as an indentured servant. Her work was often drudgery rather than training for a skilled trade. At the end of her contract—perhaps three, four, or as many as ten years—she was released. Her due payment—her *only* payment—might be a new pair of shoes and stockings or a petticoat and a white linen cap. Indentured girls were usually not allowed to marry, for that would violate the contract.

The daughters of Mary Coates were fortunate, therefore, that their mother became a shopkeeper because then she was not pressed by law or Christian responsibility to put out her girls to work. But work they did, no doubt for her in the shop. For twenty years, she ran her husband's business, importing goods from other countries, trading with other merchants, and selling to the general public. When Mary died on the eve of the American Revolution, her daughters took over the business.

Widows who were not so independent had little choice under common law but to send their children away. Even babies were indentured. If a mother refused, the court could intervene, and often did, as these colonial records from North Carolina and Virginia reveal:

NOVEMBER, 1702. MARTHA PLATO BINDS HER DAUGHTER HESTER PLATO TO CAPT. JAMES COLES AND MARY HIS WIFE TILL SHE COMES OF AGE OR MARRIES SHE BEING NOW SIX YEARS OF AGE . . .

APRIL 10, 1771. ORDERED THAT THE WIDOW BRUNLEY BE SUMMONED TO NEXT COURT TO SHOW CAUSE WHY HER CHILDREN SHALL NOT BE BOUND OUT ACCORDING TO LAW.[3]

All this was before the coming of machines. In the 1700s, America was still very much a wilderness. Most families lived on farms and made a living from working the land. While the colonists were fighting a revolution for freedom, however, a revolution of a different kind was happening in England. Machines were changing the land and the life of the people. Women had long been spinning flax into linen by hand. Now new machines were doing the work faster and more efficiently. With the coming of machines also came factories and mills. The machines could not run themselves, and so men and women and children left their farms in the country and moved to the mill towns and cities to work.

In America, the coming of machines was controversial. Stories of poverty and cruel child labor had drifted over the ocean from England. Children there were forced to work in dark and dirty mills, sometimes for as little as a half-penny an hour. From six in the morning till seven at night they tended machines, often without rest or time to eat. And what little food they had was never enough. If they were late to work, they were beaten or strapped. The children couldn't read or write. England was rapidly becoming the "workshop of the world" but at a terrible price to the welfare of the family and the children, or so many American colonists believed.

Thomas Jefferson opposed industrial development. He feared that machines would create a nation of uneducated paupers. Alexander Hamilton, on the other hand, believed industry was necessary for America to grow and prosper. Men, of course, were still needed to farm the land, he conceded. But women and, in particular, female children, he argued, could work in the mills and "render themselves more useful than they otherwise would be."

America had won its freedom from England but as long as Americans were dependent on British manufactured goods, they were not really free at all. And so, the Industrial Revolution spread, slowly at first, crossing the ocean in the early 1800s and taking root first along the gushing streams and rivers of New England.

Stitches in Time

Sarah Trask was a young woman living in the seacoast town of Lynn, Massachusetts, in the 1840s. L.W. was the man Sarah favored, a sailor who had gone to sea. When he returned, they might wed. In the meantime, she "rendered herself useful" by stitching by hand the leather "uppers" of shoes. She worked alone at home under the "putting out" system. A merchant in a delivery wagon brought the cut pieces of leather to her and picked up those she had already sewn. It was good work for a single girl. Once married, however, good girls quit working and served their husbands instead.

In her diary, Sarah revealed the loneliness and tediousness of the stitching.

> JAN 31 1849 . . . WINTER SEEM SO DULL. AT HOME ALL DAY AND IN THE EVENING. OH MY SHOES THEY DO GO OFF SO SLOW ONLY FOUR PAIRS AND A HALF TODAY, I WISH THEY WERE ALL DONE, BUT WHAT IS THE USE OF THAT IT WILL NOT GET THEM DONE ANY SOONER; SO I MUST NOT DESPAIR. . . .

Her diary reveals something more—Sarah's uncertain feelings about becoming a wife. Although in fun she sarcastically calls herself an "old maid," she also fears that fate.

> FEB 5 . . . THREE BROTHERS AND TWO SISTERS I HAVE AND AFTER LIZZY IS MARRIED, THERE WILL BE A BACHELOR AND OLD MAID LEFT. NEVER MIND, THE HAPPY LIFE THAT EVER WAS HAD IS ALWAYS TO COURT AND NEVER TO WED . . .
>
> FEB 20 . . . JUST FOR FUN I COUNTED THE STITCHES IN A SHOE, THE SIZE WAS FIVES, 719 IN THE WHOLE, 250 ON THE TOP, 173 IN THE FILLING, 120, ON THE SIDE SEAMS OR 65 IN ONE SIDE, 69 IN THE CLOSEING OR 23 ON A SEAM, 58 IN THE LINEING, OR 29, ON A SIDE, 99 ON THE SURGEING. . . .
>
> FEB 19 . . . LIZZY . . . WILL BE A BRIDE, THEN SHE MUST GO JUST WHERE HER HUSBAND SAYS . . . UNTILL HE CAN GET A HOUSE, THEN A HOME OF THEIR OWN . . . AND MAY IT BE A HAPPY ONE . . . .

Marriage to me seem a great responsibility for then you must act for yourself, and almost all the care come upon the wife. . . .

March 14 . . . Another wedding last night one of our shop girls, all getting married. Mr. Shale [the shoe boss] will not have any to work for him, if they go so fast as they have done, this two or three years.

The "putting out" system often meant long, lonely, tedious hours of work.

Despite her doubts about marriage, she scolded herself for being impatient in wishing for L.W.'s return.

May 22 . . . No news from L.W. yet, and I am almost discourage it seem as though I have look for news a year; I think some times I will not think of it, but I cannot help it, it will come up in my mind, But this will never do for me, and so I will not write my wicked thoughts, always complaining if things are not just so, Oh what a wicked girl I am . . . [4]

Many miles to the north of Lynn was the city of Lowell, where thousands of farm girls had gone to operate the spinning and weaving machines in the new factories that had been built along the Merrimack River. Lucy Larcom was one of those girls. At eleven, she had gone to work in one of the Lowell factories to help her mother make ends meet after the death of Lucy's father. She began as a "doffer" in the spinning room. The machines spun thread onto bobbins—hundreds of bobbins, row after row of bobbins. Lucy's task was to replace the full bobbins with empty ones. The work was easy enough for a little girl, but no less boring than Sarah's stitching. As she grew older, Lucy took other jobs in the factory. Then at the age of twenty-two, Lucy changed her life completely. She quit her job as a factory girl, moved to Illinois, and went to school. A few years later, she returned to Massachusetts as a teacher and a writer. One of her poems was about a girl named Hannah. Lucy Larcom never met Sarah Trask and yet Hannah's story is much like hers.

Poor lone Hannah,
Sitting at the window, binding shoes:
Faded, wrinkled,
Sitting, stitching in a mournful muse.
Bright-eyed beauty once was she,
When the bloom was on the tree:
Spring and winter,
Hannah's at the window, binding shoes.

Hannah's work, like Sarah's, is monotonous. Like Sarah Trask, too, Hannah is waiting for a lover to return from the sea to marry her and take her away from her life of work. She will wait forever.

Whispering hoarsely, "Fishermen,
Have you, have you heard of Ben?"
Old with watching,
Hannah's at the window, binding shoes.[5]

Lucy Larcom seems to ridicule girls like Sarah Trask for never leaving the window, for stitching and stitching year after year, growing old waiting for a husband to take her away. But then Lucy Larcom was not typical of most factory girls. Few advanced as she had beyond their giant machines—the power looms and the spinning frames.

A Valuable Cargo of Females

About the time that Lucy Larcom published her poem a new machine came to Lynn. It was a sewing machine that stitched leather. One girl operating a single machine could do the work of eleven Hannahs. The invention put hand stitchers like Sarah Trask out of work. Assuming that

L.W. had not returned, Sarah would have been faced with a choice: purchase one of the expensive machines and continue working in her home, or go to work in a factory that housed hundreds of sewing machines. The second choice meant lower wages and a new skill, though an easy one, to learn: working the foot treadle that operated the machine.

A few years later, this innovation was replaced by still another machine. Powered by steam and not women's feet, its stitches were straight and regular and even more swiftly sewn. Hannah's human fingers—and Sarah Trask's, too—simply could not compete.

All sorts of machines now were turning and spinning, cutting and pressing. Sewing machines stitched not only leather shoes but also straw brooms and leather-bound books. Power looms spun silk into ribbon, stockings, and

Background: East view of Lowell, Massachusetts, 1844. Left: Massachusetts textile mill girls with shuttles and reed hooks, tools they used in their work

bloomers. Cutting machines sliced through multiple thicknesses of fabric. Pressing machines stamped out 2,500 tin cans a day, as well as breadboxes, pail handles, and fasteners. Always with the machines came the factory buildings and the need for girls to work in them.

The girls were not always easily found. Factory agents traveled the New England countryside, looking for them. One Massachusetts newspaper announced that "a valuable cargo, consisting of 50 females, was recently imported into this State . . . Twenty of this number were consigned to Mann's factory at Franklin and the remaining 30 were sent to Lowell and Nashua." That women were described as cargo shipped to factories reveals how they were viewed as workers; their education and their skill mattered little, if at all. They were called "operatives," another term suggesting that the girls were little more than a sprocket in a machine.

The operatives lived in boardinghouses, eating and sleeping together as a society of working girls. In the evening after long hours tending the machines, many girls attended lectures or visited Self-Improvement Social Clubs. By ten o'clock at night, however, they were expected to be in their beds. A girl who did not comply with the rules was let go.

The coming of machines brought long hours, even in the dark of winter. At four-thirty in the morning, bells rang to wake the operatives for breakfast. By six-thirty, they were at their machines. Bells summoned them to dinner and bells released them at six-thirty in the evening. The "lighting up" time began in the autumn when the girls worked by lamplight in the morning before the sun had risen and again in the late afternoon after the sun had set. "Blow out" day was a sort of celebration, a day in March when the lamps were shut off for the season. Then the factory girls hung flowers and garlands over the lamps near their machines.

Still, the work was considered good for the girls. A newspaper article in the *Lynn Reporter* took its readers inside the factories to reveal the marvels of the new machines:

> . . . HERE WE ARE IN THE THIRD STORY OF ONE OF THE MOST FLOURISHING SHOE MANUFACTORIES IN THE CITY. HERE, IN A LARGE, WELL-LIGHTED ROOM SIT SOME THIRTY, FORTY OR FIFTY YOUNG WOMEN, NOT LANGUIDLY BENDING OVER A PIECE OF WORK FOR WHICH THEY WILL RECEIVE PERHAPS A PITTANCE . . . BUT BEFORE A MAGIC LITTLE SEWING-MACHINE, DRIVEN BY STEAM POWER . . .
>
> AND SO THEY WORK AND SING AND SMILE FROM DAY TO DAY, SOME OF THEM EARNING TEN OR TWELVE DOLLARS PER WEEK . . .

*L*etters From Susan

Not all workers were singing the praises of the factory system. A labor publication called the *Voice of Industry* questioned the accuracy of the articles that showed girls singing at their machines and earning small fortunes. If the work is so good, the *Voice of Industry* asked, then why aren't the daughters of the factory owners and the agents and superintendents working the power looms and steam-driven sewing machines? Why aren't *they* standing twelve hours a day in the lint-filled air of the carding room?

The girls themselves began to question the goodness of the work. An operative known only as Susan wrote letters to her friend Mary at home. The letters were published in *The Lowell Offering,* a literary magazine written by the factory girls. Like many operatives, Susan entered the factory and began her new life with a sense of adventure and excitement.

DEAR MARY: WHEN I LEFT HOME I TOLD YOU THAT I WOULD WRITE IN A WEEK, AND LET YOU HAVE MY FIRST IMPRESSION OF LOWELL. . . .

I ARRIVED HERE SAFE AND SOUND, AFTER BEING WELL JOLTED OVER THE ROCKS AND HILLS OF NEW HAMPSHIRE; AND WHEN (IT WAS THEN EVENING) A GENTLEMAN IN THE STAGE FIRST POINTED OUT LOWELL TO ME, WITH ITS LIGHTS TWINKLING THROUGH THE GLOOM, I COULD THINK OF NOTHING BUT PASSAMPSCOT SWAMP, WHEN BRILLIANTLY ILLUMINATED BY "LIGHTNING BUGS." . . . IT ALL APPEARS VERY ROMANTIC TO ME.

In her second letter, Susan wrote nothing of fireflies and romance. She had settled into a daily routine, controlled by bells and whirring spindles.

AT FIRST THE HOURS SEEMED VERY LONG, BUT I WAS SO INTERESTED IN LEARNING THAT I ENDURED IT VERY WELL; AND WHEN I WENT OUT AT NIGHT THE SOUND OF THE MILL WAS IN MY EARS, AS OF CRICKETS, FROGS, AND JEWSHARPS ALL MINGLED TOGETHER IN STRANGE DISCORD. . . .

IT MAKES MY FEET ACHE AND SWELL TO STAND SO MUCH, BUT I SUPPOSE I SHALL GET ACCUSTOMED TO THAT TOO. . . .

LOWELL OFFERING

December, 1845.

"Is Saul also among the prophets?"

A REPOSITORY
OF ORIGINAL ARTICLES, WRITTEN BY
"FACTORY GIRLS."

LOWELL: MISSES CURTIS & FARLEY.
BOSTON: JORDAN & WILEY, 121
Washington street.
1845.

The Lowell Offering, *December 1845*

YOU ASK IF THE WORK IS NOT DISAGREEABLE. NOT WHEN ONE
IS ACCUSTOMED TO IT. IT TIRED MY PATIENCE SADLY AT FIRST, AND
IT DOES NOW WHEN IT DOES NOT RUN WELL; BUT IN GENERAL, I
LIKE IT VERY MUCH. IT IS EASY TO DO, AND DOES NOT REQUIRE
VERY VIOLENT EXERTION, AS MUCH OF OUR FARM WORK DOES.

Weeks passed. Spring warmed into summer, apparently without another letter from Susan. Mary must have been concerned for in Susan's third letter, she offered an apology. Machines might have been magic for a newspaper reporter who toured a new factory, but machines held no wonder for one who stood before them twelve hours a day.

YOU COMPLAIN THAT I DO NOT KEEP MY PROMISE OF BEING A
GOOD CORRESPONDENT, BUT IF YOU COULD KNOW HOW SULTRY IT
IS HERE, AND HOW FATIGUED I AM BY MY WORK IN THIS WARM
WEATHER, YOU WOULD NOT BLAME ME. IT IS NOW THAT I BEGIN
TO DISLIKE THESE HOT BRICK PAVEMENTS, AND GLARING
BUILDINGS. I WANT TO BE AT HOME—TO GO DOWN THE BROOK
OVER WHICH THE WILD GRAPES HAVE MADE A NATURAL ARBOR . . ." [6]

In the mid-1800s, machines were magic and women were cargo. In the years ahead, industry and the factory system would continue to spread west to New York, Pennsylvania, and Illinois, and south to the Carolinas. Both Alexander Hamilton and Thomas Jefferson were proved correct in their opposing predictions: The coming of machines would bring great wealth to some and misery to many.

The children are playing a game. Two girls make
arches with their hands, palms to palms. The other
girls pass underneath and sing:

The needle's eye
That doth supply
The thread that runs so true;
Ah! many a lass
Have I let pass
Because I wanted . . . you!

All at once the arches fall, trapping the unlucky
player in the eye of the needle.

WPA LIFE HISTORIES, "SINGING GAMES"

A young girl, taught by her supervisor, learns
to tend a spinning machine, 1909.

CHAPTER TWO

In the Eye of the Needle

Ireland was starving. The Rooney family sold their tiny cottage and the few livestock they had and counted enough coins to buy passage for themselves and their three daughters on board a ship bound for America. Winifred Rooney was about five years old at the time of the potato famine in 1845 that so devastated Ireland. During the crossing, her father died of ship fever. The mother and her three little girls found themselves in New York City, penniless and alone.

Somehow they survived. At seven, Winifred worked as a maid. At eleven years old, she earned a dollar a week doing work for a dressmaker. As she grew a little older, she entered the factory, working for Seligman's in New York City sewing shirts and underwear. At the age of twenty-seven, she married an Irishman named O'Reilly. Unlike the good girls of Lowell years earlier who left work after marriage, Winifred could not quit her job. The O'Reillys needed all the money they could earn to pay for rent and food. Winifred gave birth to a son. When he died before his first birthday, Winifred blamed herself. She was convinced the baby had died because "she couldn't give him the attention he needed." Soon she was pregnant again and delivered in February 1870 a healthy baby girl whom she named Leonora.

For a while, life was full of hope. Winifred and her husband took all the money they had and bought a grocery store. But the business venture failed and soon after, O'Reilly died. At thirty-one, Winifred Rooney O'Reilly was right where her mother had been when she landed in America—penniless and alone.

The Immigrants

Before families like the Rooneys came to America, factory girls—especially in New England—were mostly American-born, the daughters of farming families. Most could read and write. "The girls that I room with are all from Vermont and good girls too," wrote Mary S. Paul in a letter to her father.

In the 1850s, however, a change occurred. Thousands of immigrant families were arriving in America. Like the Rooneys, they were fleeing a famished Ireland. The mothers took what work they could find. They scrubbed floors. They picked rags. Within a few years, their daughters, like Winifred, were tending factory looms and sewing machines. The American-born operatives complained about the immigrants. The immigrants weren't as well educated. They worked for lower wages. At the same time, overseers were demanding that operatives tend four and five looms instead of just two. Many of the American girls married and quit work or otherwise returned to their farming communities. They left behind an open door for the immigrants, who eagerly took their places on the factory floors.

Winifred O'Reilly went back to Seligman's, carrying little Nora with her in a laundry basket. This she set on the floor near her feet while she worked. When Nora was older, Winifred left her at home in the care of a neighbor or a friend. Some mornings the child clung to her mother, crying so loudly that Winifred could hear her even after she had walked out the

Irish immigrants leaving Queenstown Harbor in Ireland

door and started down the street. Winifred worked the long hours expected of a factory girl—no matter that she had a child waiting for her in the house on Second Avenue. Often, she carried bundles of clothing home with her to sew in the evening.

More than anything, Winifred wanted her daughter to get an education, to have a chance at a better life. Nora started school, but at about age twelve, she followed in her mother's footsteps and went to work in a factory. One day, Leonora O'Reilly would leave factory life behind to become a crusader for all working girls. With her powerful speeches, she would earn a place for herself in the pages of women's labor history. For the time being, though, she accepted without question the responsibility of helping her mother make ends meet. She was a good girl, and she went to work.

The Irish weren't the only immigrants flooding into America. By the late 1800s and early 1900s, thousands more had come—from French Canada, Germany, Italy, and Jewish villages in Russia and Poland. While their languages were different, their reasons for coming were similar. They came to escape poverty or religious persecution.

Marie-Anne was one of them. She remembered vividly a morning before her family left Canada. She had traveled with her father into the village while he made arrangements for transportation to America. In the general store, he told Mr. B, the store owner, of his plans. He was selling his land and going to make money working in a cotton mill. Marie-Anne remembered the store owner's warning:

> "Oh! No, no, don't do that, Joe," he said. ". . . You are going to make your children into slaves, spending their days behind thick, dirty walls bound to some looms in the terrific and incessant noise. From six o'clock in the morning until six o'clock at night, they will be driven by some blind power, and then, they will fall into their beds, in some crowded rooms, in order to gather enough strength to begin over again, the next day. I know! I have seen these mills, when I went for a business trip to Boston last year. I thought they were something inhuman, almost infernal. You and yours do not belong there, Joe. . . .
>
> "They will be driven like cattle; they will be 'foreigners,' they will be 'immigrants.'"[7]

The father could not be dissuaded. He was a poor man, he argued. He had struggled too long and too hard to make ends meet as a farmer. No, he had made up his mind. He was leaving.

The family settled in a New Hampshire mill town. Marie-Anne was the oldest child and soon after arriving, she went to work. If Mr. B's impassioned words about the mills alarmed her, she was powerless to do anything about it. "Girls were meek and submissive then," she said. "They did not have much to say about the arrangement of their lives."

As if she were in the child's singing game, Marie-Anne had been caught in the eye of the needle.

Life on the Lower East Side

Marie-Anne's family settled in New England, but thousands of other immigrants settled on the Lower East Side of New York City. They crowded into tenement buildings. Sometimes as many as twelve families lived in a single building. Most of the structures had not been intended to house so many families, but then New York City had not been prepared for so many immigrants. Quick to take advantage of the situation, landlords divided the apartments and rented the rooms and even the cellars to the new arrivals desperate for some place to live.

Jacob Riis was a photographer and a writer. In the 1890s, he took his readers, many of whom had never stepped foot on the Lower East Side, on a tour of a tenement on Cherry Street. A dirty white bow hung on the door, indicating that one of the families living there was mourning a death. Inside, Riis described what he saw—or rather what he experienced with his other senses, for the inside of a tenement building was always dark even in daylight hours.

> BE A LITTLE CAREFUL, PLEASE! THE HALL IS DARK AND YOU MIGHT STUMBLE OVER THE CHILDREN PITCHING PENNIES BACK THERE. . . . HERE WHERE THE HALL TURNS AND DIVES INTO UTTER DARKNESS IS A STEP, AND ANOTHER, ANOTHER. A FLIGHT OF STAIRS. YOU CAN FEEL YOUR WAY, IF YOU CANNOT SEE IT. CLOSE? YES! WHAT WOULD YOU HAVE? ALL THE FRESH AIR THAT EVER ENTERS THESE STAIRS COMES FROM THE HALLDOOR THAT IS FOREVER SLAMMING, AND FROM THE WINDOWS OF THE DARK BEDROOMS THAT IN TURN

An Italian immigrant mother and her two young children in a tenement doing piecework (in this case, shelling nuts).

RECEIVE FROM THE STAIRS THEIR SOLE SUPPLY OF THE ELEMENTS GOD MEANT TO BE FREE . . . THAT WAS A WOMAN FILLING HER PAIL BY THE HYDRANT YOU JUST BUMPED AGAINST. THE SINKS ARE IN THE HALLWAY, THAT ALL THE TENANTS MAY HAVE ACCESS— AND ALL BE POISONED ALIKE BY THEIR SUMMER STENCHES. HEAR THE PUMP SQUEAK! IT IS THE LULLABY OF TENEMENT- HOUSE BABES. IN SUMMER, WHEN A THOUSAND THIRSTY THROATS PANT FOR A COOLING DRINK IN THIS BLOCK, IT IS WORKED IN VAIN. BUT THE SALOON, WHOSE OPEN DOOR YOU PASSED IN THE HALL, IS ALWAYS THERE. THE SMELL OF IT HAS FOLLOWED YOU UP. HERE IS A DOOR. LISTEN! THAT SHORT HACKING COUGH, THAT TINY, HELPLESS WAIL—WHAT DO THEY MEAN? THEY MEAN THAT THE SOILED BOW OF WHITE YOU SAW ON THE DOOR DOWNSTAIRS WILL HAVE ANOTHER STORY TO TELL—OH! A SADLY FAMILIAR STORY—BEFORE THE DAY IS AT AN END. THE CHILD IS DYING WITH MEASLES. WITH HALF A CHANCE IT MIGHT HAVE LIVED; BUT IT HAD NONE. THAT DARK BEDROOM KILLED IT. [8]

Bella Spewack was only three years old when she arrived in America from Transylvania with her mother, who had divorced. Her mother worked in the needle trades. She was a seamstress and she sewed in the front room of their tenement apartment, the only room with windows. She took in boarders as well, mostly Hungarian servant girls, Bella remembered. For ten cents a night, the girls shared a bed or, if that was already full, slept in the same bed with Bella and her mother. At times, male boarders slept in the kitchen on folding beds or on the floor. Bella despised her mother's boarders and yet their daily dimes helped to keep Bella in school, out of the factories, and out of the eye of the needle.

Life in a Southern Mill Village

Not all working girls lived in crowded city tenement buildings. In the mountains of Pennsylvania and North and South Carolina, other girls were growing up in the shadows of coal breakers (buildings where coal from the mine was broken up and sorted) and cotton mills. They were the daughters of miners or poor southern farmers who, after some misfortune, had given up the land and went to work in the mills. These girls lived in the coal patches and mill villages in company houses. Most were four-room shanties—called "shotgun shacks" in some southern towns—built by the owners of the mines and the mills as cheap housing for their workers.

When a reporter for the Federal Writers' Project came to the mill village of East Durham, North Carolina, in the 1930s, Juanita Hinson offered to show the writer around. To an outsider, the community was like so many other mill towns: the shacks gray with soot from the many trains that transported materials to and from the factories; the front yards bare of grass; the streets muddy in winter and chokingly dusty in summer. As Juanita began her tour on Reservoir Street, no doubt she voiced what the reporter was privately thinking.

THESE HOUSES AIN'T WORTH MUCH, ARE THEY? YOU NOTICE HOW OLD THEY LOOK FROM THE OUTSIDE? WELL, THEY LOOK WORSE ON THE INSIDE. THE FLOORS ARE SPLINTERY AND THE WALLS ARE SO AWFUL DINGY.

Through Juanita's eyes, though, the reporter began to see beyond the shabbiness of the shacks. In the eye of the girl was beauty, even in East Durham.

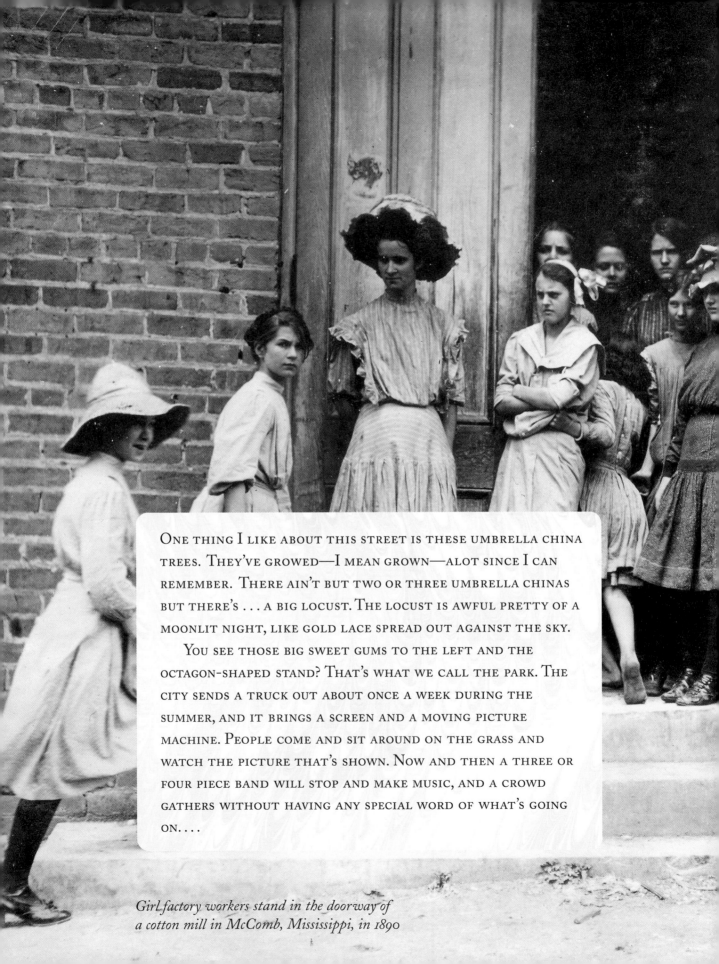

One thing I like about this street is these umbrella china trees. They've growed—I mean grown—alot since I can remember. There ain't but two or three umbrella chinas but there's . . . a big locust. The locust is awful pretty of a moonlit night, like gold lace spread out against the sky.

You see those big sweet gums to the left and the octagon-shaped stand? That's what we call the park. The city sends a truck out about once a week during the summer, and it brings a screen and a moving picture machine. People come and sit around on the grass and watch the picture that's shown. Now and then a three or four piece band will stop and make music, and a crowd gathers without having any special word of what's going on. . . .

Girl factory workers stand in the doorway of a cotton mill in McComb, Mississippi, in 1890

Juanita earned extra money by helping her mother tag tobacco each day after school. They sat together on the front stoop for two or three hours. For every ten thousand tags Juanita twisted onto the sacks, she received seventy-five cents. She wanted to quit school, she told the government reporter, and work all the time. Her older sister Christine had quit two years earlier to work in the mill. But now Christine was dead set against Juanita making the same mistake.

CHRISTINE SAYS I'LL REGRET IT ALL MY LIFE IF I QUIT. MAYBE I WOULD LATER ON BUT THERE'D BE NOTHING TO REGRET RIGHT NOW. IT'S AWFUL TO HAVE TO SIT IN A ROOM WHERE MOST OF THE PEOPLE HAVE ON GOOD CLOTHES AND YOU ARE SO ASHAMED OF YOUR OWN. IT'S AWFUL TO SEE YOUR TEACHER GET UP WITH A SLIP IN HER HAND AND TO KNOW THAT IN A MINUTE SHE'LL BE READING YOUR NAME OUT AS ONE THAT HASN'T PAID THE BOOK RENT. I HATED MY TEACHER LAST YEAR FOR DOIN' JUST THAT. SHE'D SAY, "IT'S JUST 85 [CENTS] A TERM AND I DON'T SEE WHY YOU CAINT PAY."

SOME FOLKS DON'T KNOW THAT WHEN YOU HAVEN'T GOT IT 85 CENTS IS JUST AS HARD TO PAY AS A HUNDRED DOLLARS. . . . [9]

Girls like Juanita were also caught in the eye of the needle. Their fathers' wages were not enough to support the family. And so Juanita, like Leonora O'Reilly, faced a difficult choice between school and work. For many girls, it wasn't really a choice at all. They went to work—but not for the good of the industry or for their own moral development. They went to work for the good of the family.

I'd better be gettin' home so' I can help Mama tag bulls, Juanita told the reporter. *That'll help to buy bread.*

—*how many cents a day?*
How many cents for the sleepy eyes and fingers?

CARL SANDBURG, MILL DOORS

Seamstresses are busy at work as their male foremen stand watch

CHAPTER THREE

Cents a Day

Working girls lived by their fingers. Fingers picked and cleaned nuts, separating the whole meats from the broken pieces of shells. Fingers knotted together the short, scraggy ends of ostrich feathers (a practice known as willowing) to make long, graceful plumes for women's hats and dresses.

The faster her fingers worked, the more cents a girl earned. In a nut factory in New York City, a dozen Italian girls sat at a long table. The factory provided no chairs, just boxes on which the girls could sit. With fingers that quickly became dirty, they sorted and then packed nuts into glass jars and boxes that were then transported (without any further disinfecting) to groceries and candy stores. The factory paid the girls six cents a pound. Two girls, working together, might clean fifteen pounds in three hours. After dividing the ninety cents between them, the girls had earned just fifteen cents an hour.

In a Chicago feather factory there were huge bins filled with feathers from all kinds of barnyard birds—chickens, hens, and roosters. The mounds nearly reached the bare rafters, which were thick with cobwebs and feather particles. The air, too, was dusty from the down. Here little Annie's dimpled fingers rapidly sorted the feathers by body part: wing feathers in one box, tail feathers in another, breast feathers in still another box. Feathers stuck to her hair and to her clothing. She squinted from the dust as her fingers worked. The factory paid Annie between seven and ten cents for each pound of feathers she sorted. She was a quick worker and could sort as much as thirteen pounds of feathers a day.

Willowing paid more, at least for a time: fifteen cents per inch. Once more girls learned how to willow and competition increased, the rate dropped to three cents. A single ostrich plume might have more than 8,600 knots—123 per inch. In the early 1900s, fingers that willowed earned a single penny for every 41 knots.

The Wage-Earning Girls of Wilkes-Barre

In 1915, Sarah Atherton completed a study of wage-earning girls under the age of sixteen in Wilkes-Barre, Pennsylvania, for the National Child Labor Committee (NCLC). For more than ten years, the NCLC had been fighting to pass child labor laws. One goal of the committee was to ban child labor under the age of fourteen and, in dangerous occupations, under the age of sixteen. To further their argument that *not all work* was good for children, they needed statistics. Sarah Atherton agreed to go into the mills and factories of her home-

A feather boa was part of many well-dressed ladies' outfits in 1910.

40

town, to speak with the working girls, and to visit with their families in their homes. She opened the first chapter of her survey with this description:

> ONCE THE WYOMING VALLEY WAS COVERED WITH UNBROKEN FOREST, THE HORIZON WAS CLEAR EXCEPT FOR THE WRAITH-LIKE SMOKE OF STRAY INDIAN CAMP FIRES.
>
> LATER IT WAS PLANTED WITH FARMS AND ORCHARDS. THERE AROSE THE SMOKE FROM CHIMNEYS OF THE EARLY CONNECTICUT SETTLERS. NOW IT IS FILLED FROM END TO END WITH MINING TOWNS. THE HORIZON, NIGHT OR DAY, IS NEVER FREE FROM WHITE SMOKE AND STEAM.

The smoke and steam came, in part, from coal breakers. At the turn of the century, Wilkes-Barre was the center of the anthracite coal region. Smoke and steam came also from the mills that had followed the coal mines into the valley, hoping to employ the wives and children of the miners. The mills produced all types of textiles and metal: silks, cottons, laces, and tin. That the horizon was never free from the smoke indicated that the factories operated late into the night. The owners of the coal mines, the railroads, and the Kirby-Woolworth dimestore chain lived in elegant mansionlike homes on wide elm-lined avenues along the Susquehanna River. Their workers lived away from them, in coal patches where company shanties squatted one close to the other.

What Sarah Atherton observed and later wrote about in her survey "haunted" her. The worn and dirty factory floors, the lack of fresh air, even the smell of the silk distressed her. She wrote of her visit to a cotton mill:

> IN A COTTON MILL THE TEMPERATURE HAS TO BE HIGH ON ACCOUNT OF THE THIN THREADS. IT WAS A RAINY DAY IN MAY, AND THE TEMPERATURE IN THE MILL WAS 85 DEGREES FAHRENHEIT. ADD TO THIS A ROAR OF MACHINERY SO DEAFENING THAT ONE HAS TO SCREAM

Atherton's study showed that the grade level of school a girl had completed made little or no difference to the wage she earned. A girl who left school in the seventh or eighth grade earned no more than a girl who had completed only the fourth or fifth grade of school. Nor were years of work experience a guarantee of an increase in wages. The reason, explained Atherton, was the mechanical nature of the work. The factory system had divided the labor into single acts. One girl cleaned and sorted nuts, for example, while another packed them into jars. One girl, like Annie, sorted feathers while another split them and still another willowed. For most girls, the only hope of earning higher wages was to complete faster, if possible, the mechanical motions of their fingers. Atherton watched the girls as they worked:

IN THE TIN MILL ONE WORKER MAKES 500
METAL TOPS AN HOUR. WHEN ASKED HOW
MANY, A GIRL AT AN IMPRESSION MACHINE
REPLIED, "NOT MANY, IT'S SLOW ON ACCOUNT
OF THE MAGNET—ABOUT 200 AN HOUR." THE

Girls wind silk at the looms of the Sauquoit Silk Manufacturing Company in Pennsylvania in 1918.

43

PROCESS INCLUDED PUTTING A CAN HELD BY A LONG MAGNET INTO A MACHINE, PRESSING IT, TAKING IT OUT; TWO HUNDRED AN HOUR WAS "SLOW." SIXTY TO SIXTY-FIVE TWO-FOOT CANS ARE SOLDERED IN ONE HOUR.

IT IS GENERALLY BELIEVED THAT THE GIRLS WORK VERY MECHANICALLY. JUST HOW MECHANICALLY IS ILLUSTRATED BY THE FOLLOWING: ONE GIRL WAS ASKED, "HOW LONG HAVE YOU WORKED HERE?"

"SIX YEARS."

"WHAT ARE THE LITTLE TOPS YOU ARE MAKING FOR?"

"I REALLY DON'T KNOW."

In the same tin mill, another girl fed a stamping machine. Her single task was to cut and press fasteners for bucket handles. With her right foot she shoved the treadle. Down came the stamp. She moved the tin about under the stamp, cutting the entire sheet, "like using all the dough when stamping out biscuits," observed Atherton. She described the girl as "resistant and angular as the sheet of tin in her hands." Over and over she repeated the motion, cutting eight to ten thousand fasteners a day, each time always careful not to stamp her fingers as well as the tin.

Atherton's study gave the NCLC valuable statistics. Her experience in researching the report gave her something more—a memory that she couldn't quite put out of her mind. Some of the factory girls looked happy, she admitted. Far more, she added, did not. "Some of them are so stoop-shouldered," she wrote, "as to look as though they had been carrying millstones about their necks."

The sight of the ever-present smoke and steam on the horizon was a sad reminder of what she had seen inside the mills. "There can never be quite silenced the hum of that machinery," she wrote, "the picture will not be utterly erased of hands that go back and forth through hours, days and years."[10]

Mechanical Motions

The mechanical motions of the wage-earning girls of Wilkes-Barre were duplicated in factories and mills in cities across the country. Inside a Pittsburgh cracker factory a girl sat beside a large roller. Her only task was to brush flour over the thin sheets of dough moving slowly past her on a conveyor belt. Hers was a single motion repeated perhaps a hundred times an hour, a thousand times a day, all the while requiring her to concentrate on the continuously moving carrier. On another floor in the same factory, a girl gathered the just-baked biscuits as they came to her on a moving belt and packed them in boxes. In still another department, a girl breathing hard through gritted teeth, as if—one observer remarked—she were running a race, rapidly folded the corners of a cracker box. She reached for another, folded; reached for another, folded. She earned a penny a dozen. If she folded a hundred dozen in a single day, the company would pay her a ten-cent bonus. Most girls did not earn the bonus.

A single motion—like dusting flour or peeling hot biscuits from a moving conveyor—could be learned within minutes. But quickly repeating the same motion over and over again often meant training the muscles to keep pace with a machine's slapping belts or moving chains. The girls did not control the speed of the machine. The machine controlled the speed of their fingers.

Aggressive foremen or floorwalkers also ensured that the girls kept pace with the machines. Inside the National Biscuit Company factory in New York City, Anna Saitta's fingers bled from the hot crackers that stuck to the pan. The conveyor belt did not slow for bleeding fingers. Anna worked a few feet from the glowing cracker ovens. Even when girls fainted, the moving belts did not slow or stop.

The heat was terrible, Anna said. *The foreman was every five minutes hollering at us today, because we couldn't work fast. . . . The foreman is always snooping around telling us to work faster or we will get canned today.*[11]

"No girl can keep up her pace more than six years," a manager of a stogie (cigar) factory once remarked to an outsider who watched girls strip-

Oyster shuckers at work

ping tobacco and rolling it into small cigars. Sarah Cohen worked in this factory. When she was sixteen, she could strip and roll stogies so swiftly she earned twelve dollars a week. At twenty-one, she could not roll many more than fourteen pounds a week. Her fingers had slowed and her wages had dropped to less than a dollar a day. Girls with slow fingers, girls with old fingers were not kept on very long by factory foremen.

Girls lived by their fingers and their fingers showed the scars of their work. In fish canning factories, women and children shucked oysters, standing all day alongside rail cars full of the steaming shellfish. With a knife, they pried opened the partially cooked oysters, slicing out the meat and dropping it into a pail. The empty shells accumulated in a brittle pile under their feet and over their ankles. The shells—not the knife—cut their fingers until they swelled and then bled. The wage was weighed in pailsful of oysters—four pounds for a nickel was considered by many cannery foremen to be a fair price. A child of six or seven might shuck and fill four pails a day. Her older sister or mother might double that amount.

Shrimp, on the other hand, were spread in ice over wire mesh trays. The worker broke off the heads then squeezed the flesh from the shell. A doctor commenting on the ammonia burns from the shellfish admitted that the acid "irritates the skin quite badly, but . . . the hands become hardened and toughened to it."

Ella Merryvale quit school in the sixth grade to work in a Florida fruit-canning factory. Ella's work required a mechanical motion using a "sectionizer knife" for which the plant charged her seventy-five cents. During her first weeks, the acid from the flesh of the oranges and grapefruit burned the skin from her fingers.

In laundries, vats of boiling water and starch filled the room with steam. Windows could not be opened for then the cinders and dirt from the streets would dirty the just-washed clothes. Without fresh air, the girls breathed in the fumes of soda from the detergents, ammonia from the starches, and gas from the hot irons. Here in the steamy atmosphere, women often removed their blouses while they worked. Mangle operators threaded the clothes through the large rollers meant to squeeze out the excess water. The machines were called manglers for the obvious reason: The rollers could crush fingers, hands, and arms. Ironers pressed the laundry by manually pushing the heavy irons, a shirt a minute. *I'd come home of a night feelin' like my arms was clean loose from the sockets,* Lucille Hicks remembered.[12] She began work in the fifth grade. Other girls ironed by using their feet as well as their hands, operating gas-fired rollers. The bottom roller served as an ironing board. The top roller, heated by gas jets, was the iron. The girls operated the rollers with foot treadles. For ten or twelve hours a day—longer if a rush was on—they stood and treaded the heavy rollers. They earned about six dollars a week.

Mr. G's Coat Shop

One summer morning, on assignment from the Chicago *Times*, a woman journalist who used the name "Nell Nelson" dressed "down," meaning quite simply, and left her home to seek work in the factories of Chicago. She carried with her a list of employment places in the city: feather factories, candy factories, sewing shops. Her challenge was to get hired and work at whatever tasks were assigned to her, all the while observing the girls around her, and then write about what she saw. The *Times* would then publish her articles in a series exposing the conditions under which the girls of Chicago worked. Above all, Nell Nelson was to keep her true identity a secret, even from the girls themselves.

On her first day, Nell was turned away from a candy factory and two corset shops. She found work in a feather factory where she met "little Annie," who taught Nell how to distinguish tail feathers from breast feathers and side feathers. Nell thought she would suffocate in that gloomy, dusty room where by noon feathers covered her and stuck to her lips. On another day, she found work in one of the many sewing factories in Chicago. Her machine was steam powered, and Nell could not handle it. The power was supplied to the machines by a switch that the foreman alone operated. A girl could not turn her machine off or on as she wished, but she could control its speed by pressing her knee—hard—against the starting wheel. "I pressed my knee against the starting wheel to make it go slow until the buckle on my garter got red hot." Even then, her fingers had difficulty keeping the stitches straight and even.[13]

Nell soon learned that a working girl's wage was subjected to various operating charges and fines. In some sewing factories, girls were forced to purchase the needles and oil for their machines. Some were required to rent the daily use of the company's machines, paying for the steam power that drove the motors. These charges cut into the cents earned each day. Then there were the fines levied for breaking the factory's rules. Some rules were stated outright and understood. A sign posted on the wall of one sewing factory warned: *Ladies and Gentlemen it is in your interest and that of your neighbors that no talking is allowed. Whoever talks loud is fined 10 cents.* If a girl arrived late to work after the whistle had ceased, she might be sent home and lose the day's wage—plus the trolley-car fare she might have spent getting to and from work. Or, the foreman might lock her out for thirty minutes, then dock, or "pull," two hours' wages from her week's earnings.

Not all rules were put into writing but the girls understood them just the same. A girl could not leave her machine to go to the toilet whenever she wished. If she did, a forewoman followed and watched and waited. In some workshops at the end of the day, the foreman expected each girl to sweep her place and to clean and oil her machine.

One morning in July, Nell applied for work at Mr. G's coat shop. She took her place at an empty machine.

> . . . THE BOSS CAME NEAR MY CHAIR AND THREW A PLAID SACK
> COAT IN MY LAP AND WITHOUT A WORD WALKED AWAY. HERE WAS
> A NICE PREDICAMENT I THOUGHT, AS I LOOKED THE GALLEY OVER.
> I ASKED THE LITTLE YELLOW-HAIRED SWEDE GIRL AT MY RIGHT
> WHERE TO BEGIN, BUT SHE LOOKED AT ME AND RESUMED HER
> "FEELING" WITHOUT A WORD OF REPLY. THEN I ASKED A BIG,
> YELLOW-HAIRED, DOUGH-FACED GERMAN GIRL ON MY LEFT AND
> RECEIVED THE SAME KIND OF RESPONSE. INSTANTLY I REALIZED
> THEIR POSITION. COMPULSORY SILENCE.

Nell began to sew. Suddenly, Mr. G came behind her to inspect her work. He leaned so close to her that he nearly burned her cheek with his "nasty-smelling" cigar. He told her to take smaller stitches, to rip out the work she had already done, and to do it over. At noon, he left the shop, and the girls got forty minutes for lunch. With Mr. G gone, the girls were friendlier. One Jewish girl confided to Nell that she had begun work in Mr. G's coat shop two years earlier when she was twelve.

> "G. THINKS WOMEN ARE COWS, THAT THEY MUST BE DRIVEN. SO
> HE DRIVES US. WE HAVE TO BE AT WORK AT 7 IN THE MORNING
> AND STAY TILL 6 IN THE EVENING." . . .
> "WHAT IF YOU ARE SICK?"
> "IF YOU'RE SICK, HE 'PULLS' YOU. HE 'PULLED' ME FOR TWENTY
> CENTS FOR BEING LATE LAST WEEK. HE 'PULLS' ALL THE HANDS
> WHEN THEY COME LATE, AND HE 'PULLS' IF WE TALK."

Mr. G returned at a quarter to one. All conversation ceased as he once again fired up the machines.

. . . THE PLACE WAS NOISY WITH FLYING SHUTTLES, CLICKING NEEDLES, AND THE WHIZZING WHEELS OF THE ROARING MACHINERY. FAIR YOUNG HEADS AND PRETTY SHOULDERS BENT OVER HEAVY COATS, AND FACES WERE SO LOW THAT THEY ALMOST TOUCHED THE SEWING IN THE OWNERS' LAPS. THE CLATTER OF THE MACHINES WAS DEAFENING, AND EVERY NOW AND THEN THE SHOP RESOUNDED WITH THE HEAVY HOT-IRONS WIELDED BY THE PRESSERS IN THE BACK ROOM. NOBODY HAD ANY TIME TO HAND THE WORK, INSTEAD OF WHICH THE CUTTER THREW IT TO THE TRIMMER, WHO IN TURN THREW IT TO THE BASTER, AND SO IT MOVED FROM HAND TO MACHINE, GOING THE ROUND OF THE THIRTY ODD WORKERS WITH SUCH RAPIDITY THAT THE AIR SEEMED FILLED WITH FLYING COATS. THE ROOM WAS LOW, AND WITH EVERY PASSAGE OF COAT-TAIL MUFFY CLOUDS OF LINT SEEMED FLOATING ABOUT IN SPACE. ADD TO THAT POOR LIGHT, BAD VENTILATION, THE EXHALATIONS OF SO MANY PEOPLE, THE SMELL OF DYE FROM THE CLOTH, AND THE NOXIOUS ODOR OF THAT EVER-CONSUMING CIGAR AND YOU HAVE MATERIAL FOR THE MAKE-UP OF MR. G'S COAT SHOP. ALL AFTERNOON WE SEWED; SEWED INCESSANTLY WITHOUT UTTERING A SYLLABLE OR RESTING A MOMENT.

After almost a full day in Mr. G's coat shop, Nell was exhausted. Her eyes throbbed from a bad headache. She had sweated through the front of her blouse. Her hair was damp and lint coated. The workday was not over, but Nell could do no more. She tossed aside the brown chinchilla overcoat on which she had been working all day and stretched her arms and back and neck. Suddenly, Mr. G was behind her again.

GRABBING THE FRAME OF MY CHAIR HE JAMMED IT DOWN ON ALL FOURS AND TOLD ME TO "GET TO WORK."

"HOW MUCH AM I GOING TO GET FOR THIS WORK?" I
INQUIRED, AFTER RECOVERING FROM MY ASTONISHMENT AND THE
SUDDEN SHOCK OF GRAVITATION.

"DO YOU WANT TO KNOW?" HE ASKED WITH A CONTEMPTIBLY
SIGNIFICANT LAUGH..

He walked away without giving her an answer. At ten minutes past five, Nell stood and approached him at the cutting board. She demanded her wages. He tossed a twenty-five-cent piece at her. "That's what I value you at," he said.

Nell might have wished at that moment to reveal her true identity and purpose in sweating over his steam-powered sewing machine. But she did not. She took the quarter and left, determined to expose the unscrupulous Mr. G in her newspaper story.

The *Times* published her articles and later collected them into a book with a sensational title, *The White Slave Girls of Chicago*. In that book, Nell dreamed of one day using the money she had earned from the articles she had written for the *Times* to hold a shoe-and-stocking party for all the shop girls of Chicago.

"In all this wide, weary, work-a-day world," she wrote, "there is not a better, brighter, nobler girl than the one who stitches, lines, binds and vamps."[14]

Nell Nelson was really Nell Cusack, a reporter for the Chicago Times. *The newspaper published her exposé in 1888.*

The laundries I found were hurrying delicate young girls to graves. One little creature that I met on my early morning tour, whose certificate bore the age of sixteen, told me that she was only fourteen. She had already been working for two years and was considered competent to take charge of a mangle, a position tiring and perilous enough for a strong woman. Her parents were both dead and she had to depend on herself. When I looked at her delicate little figure, her thin hands and pale face, I knew it wouldn't be for long.

MARY KENNEY O'SULLIVAN[15]

"The little one is a crackerjack on spinnin', at least so the boss says….The oldest one isn't so good at it. Not as quick," said the father of Lacy (12 years old) and Savannah (11 years old) Ballard.

CHAPTER FOUR

The Investigators

In New York State in 1895, no child under the age of fourteen could work in a factory. It was a state law. The law, however, was difficult to enforce. There were too many factories and too few inspectors. When an inspector entered a workplace, the factory foreman often hid children or hurried them out back doors. Pauline Newman worked on the ninth floor of the Triangle shirtwaist factory in New York City. She was twelve but other children as young as eight worked in a section of the factory the girls called "the kindergarten." Pauline remembered how the foreman was always "tipped off" when an inspector was on the way. He made all the children climb into large boxes filled with shirts. *Then some shirts were piled on top of us,* Pauline said, *and when the inspector came—No children.*

Employers were not the only ones who broke child labor laws. Desperate parents often connived with dishonest public officials to put their daughters to work. Fanny Harris was one of those girls.

Fanny's Testimony

In 1895 the governor of New York, Levi Parsons Morton, appointed a committee to investigate the conditions of female labor in New York City. The investigation became known as the Reinhard Committee, named after its chairman, Richard J. Reinhard, Jr. After months of work, the committee made its first report. Violations of child labor laws as well as health and safety laws were "constant." Yet, the committee was faced with a problem. Many female employees were unwilling to speak freely about the conditions under which they worked. They feared losing their jobs and being blacklisted—that is, having their names put on a list of troublemakers that was then circulated to other factories, preventing the girls from getting a job elsewhere. The committee recommended holding private hearings, or sessions, where no employers were present, in order to get the whole truth.

Fanny Harris was one of the child witnesses called to testify. Fanny admitted that she didn't know for certain how old she was. She had never gone to school and she could not read or write. She worked in a factory, and each week she gave her mother the two dollars she had earned. In exchange, her mother gave Fanny an allowance of two cents to spend as she wished. The interviewer asked Fanny about her mother and the piece of paper her mother had signed saying Fanny was old enough to work.

Q.—DOES YOUR MAMMA WORK?
A.—NOW SHE AIN'T WORKING, BECAUSE I AM WORKING, BUT BEFORE, WHEN I DIDN'T WORK, SHE WORKED.
Q.—YOUR MAMMA IS NOT SICK, IS SHE?
A.—NO, SIR.

Q.—And your mamma wants you to go to work?

A.—Yes, sir; sure she does; and I want to go to work myself.

Q.—And if you don't go to work then your mamma will have to go to work?

A.—Sure.

Q.—Now, Fanny, when will you be 15 years of age?

A.—I don't know.

Q.—Are you 15 now?

A.—No, sir.

Q.—And this paper (showing age certificate) your mamma gave you, did she?

A.—I went to a lawyer and paid twenty-five cents and he gave me it . . . .[16]

Fanny was one of hundreds—perhaps thousands—of girls working illegally in the city. Their age certificates had been falsified. Many of these child workers were undersized and malnourished, dressed without warm clothing, some without shoes. Like Fanny, they were ignorant in basic schooling. They could not add or subtract numbers or spell the simplest words When the interviewer asked Fanny to spell the word "cat," Fanny said she forgot how.

Investigators of other studies in other states found similar poverty and illiteracy. In Tuscaloosa, Alabama, Mother Jones, who was a labor organizer, walked into a rope factory at ten o'clock at night. She was an elderly woman with wire-rim glasses and gray hair pinned back in a bun. The superintendent, she said, did not suspect her fact-finding mission and allowed her to move freely about. She watched two little girls tending a siding of 155 spindles. A man standing nearby admitted that the children were his. One was nine and the other, ten. The girls worked twelve hours for ten cents each per day. The father worked the same hours for thirty cents more. At dawn at the end of the shift, Mother Jones watched them leave, "half-fed, half-clothed." In her autobiography, she wrote of the abuses of child labor:

I HAVE SEEN MOTHERS TAKE THEIR BABES AND SLAP COLD WATER IN THEIR FACES TO WAKE THE POOR LITTLE THINGS. I HAVE WATCHED THEM ALL DAY LONG TENDING THE DANGEROUS MACHINERY. I HAVE SEEN THEIR HELPLESS LIMBS TORN OFF, AND THEN WHEN THEY WERE DISABLED AND OF NO MORE USE TO THE MASTER, THROWN OUT TO DIE.[17]

The Social Reformers

By the beginning of the twentieth century, society, which had once viewed work as good for the child, good for industry, even good for the family, was beginning to change its mind.

Social activist Jane Addams argued that child labor was harming, not helping, families. Discouraged fathers who could not support their families had come to rely on the work of their children to pay the bills. Other fathers, said Addams, expected their children to support them completely. Addams told the story of a grieving father from Italy whose twelve-year-old daughter had just died of illness. Addams wrote: "In his grief he said, quite simply, 'She was my oldest kid. In two years she could have supported me, and now I shall have to work five or six years longer until the next one can do it.' He expected to retire permanently at thirty-four."

As a child, John Spargo had been forced to work in the coal mines of Cornwall, England. He, too, had grown up hungry and without any formal schooling. As a young man, he educated himself and emigrated to the United

The original caption on this 1890s engraving reads: "Tired out—a factory girl's room in a tenement house."

States. In 1904 he began an investigation of his own into child labor practices. He published his findings in a book called *The Bitter Cry of the Children*. In that book, he described some of the dangerous conditions under which girls worked.

In a tanning factory, a machine tore the fur from the skin of rabbits as part of the process of making felt hats. Here Spargo watched a young girl tending the machine hour after hour, all the while breathing in thick particles of animal dander and hair.

> . . . SHE WORE A NEWSPAPER PINNED OVER HER HEAD AND A HANDKERCHIEF TIED OVER HER MOUTH. SHE WAS WHITE WITH DUST FROM HEAD TO FEET, AND WHEN SHE STOOPED TO PICK ANYTHING FROM THE FLOOR, THE DUST WOULD FALL FROM HER PAPER HEAD-COVERING IN LITTLE HEAPS. ABOUT SEVEN FEET FROM THE MOUTH OF THE MACHINE WAS A WINDOW THROUGH WHICH POURED THICK VOLUMES OF DUST AS IT WAS BELCHED OUT FROM THE MACHINE. I PLACED A SHEET OF PAPER ON THE INNER SILL OF THE WINDOW AND IN TWENTY MINUTES IT WAS COVERED WITH A LAYER OF FINE DUST; HALF AN INCH DEEP. YET THAT GIRL WORKS MIDWAY BETWEEN THE WINDOW AND THE MACHINE, IN THE VERY CENTRE OF THE VOLUME OF DUST, SIXTY HOURS A WEEK.[18]

In textile mills and print shops, he saw children working with poisonous dyes. One local physician told Spargo that the children were often "saturated" with the dangerous chemicals so that parts of their bodies were as vividly dyed as the fabrics in the machines. According to Spargo, he could track the children from the factory gates to their homes simply by following their red, blue, and green footprints in the snow.

Elizabeth Beardsley Butler, like Jane Addams and John Spargo, was a social reformer. The Russell Sage Foundation, a social organization dedicated to the improvement of living conditions for all workers, had hired her to study female laborers in Pittsburgh. Butler's study would be the first ever in the country to focus solely on women. Her research took one year to complete. During that time Butler toured more than four hundred factories—factories that manufactured food, cigars, clothing, metals and glass, boxes, brooms, caskets, and cork.

She interviewed the superintendents and floorwalkers. They allowed her into their factories, where she could observe with careful detail the skill required for the girls to complete their work. She noted their hours and their wages. In 1907, a hundred years after the coming of machines, the work was still long—ten hours, twelve hours, sometimes fourteen hours a day. And it was still cheap. The beginning wages of a girl of fourteen in Pittsburgh, Butler discovered, were one-half the wages of a boy the same age.

Each factory had its attendant health risks. In a cigar factory, Butler wrote, the air was "heavy from the nicotine exhaled by mellowing leaves and thick with the dust of pulverized scrap . . ." In a wool cleaning plant, the fumes from the chemical solvents made the girls dizzy, nauseous, or in more extreme instances caused sleeplessness or even hysteria.

In a molasses plant the floor and walls were thick and sticky from the stuff. "A visitor can scarcely walk without being fastened like a fly to whatever spot he touches," Butler wrote. Here four girls worked as a team, filling cans. The molasses came "in a continuous stream" over which the girls had no control. The stuff splattered the floor, the walls, and, of course, the girls.

Butler descended into damp cellars where old women too slow now for factory work stripped tobacco. She climbed a narrow wooden staircase without railings, open and dangerously close to running machine motors and "rapidly moving" belts and ropes, to the top floor of a factory where girls sewed mattresses. Naked lightbulbs hung from the rafters. She counted the number of windows, noted their size and whether they were open or closed. She noted the stooped postures, the pale skin, and then she moved on to the next workplace.

Manufacturing lightbulbs, too, was good work for girls. They sat at a table, staring through a colored glass at a white-hot flame, Butler reported, holding the end of a wire in the flame until it fused. "Many wear glasses," Butler reported, "but except for the colored glass on the table in front of the white flame, the company offers no protection for the eyesight of its employees."

In a painting factory, the smell of the chemical lacquers was so strong that the foremen escorting Butler could not stay in the room where the girls worked. The windows were shut to prevent soot from Pittsburgh's hundreds of smoking chimneys from blowing inside and spoiling the lacquer finish on the metals. "Does the smell bother you?" Butler asked one of the workers. The girl admitted she had headaches but said she stood the work quite well.

In garment factories, the rows of vibrating machines were connected one to the other by a revolving shaft six inches from the floor. Protective boards kept the girls' skirts from getting caught in the spinning shaft. In some factories Butler visited, no protective boards were used. Even in others where the boards were in place, a girl who bent over to pick up a dropped spool of thread could still have her hair caught in the spinning shaft and ripped out by the roots.

Elizabeth Butler submitted her report in 1908. The girls were unambitious, she concluded, but not because they were lazy. They were hired, she said, because they would work for less. And they worked for less because they lacked skills and, at times, strength. It was a vicious circle and the only way out that Butler could see was education. Until a woman could move into more skilled work, she would remain at the mercy of the machines.

Trade Diseases

John Spargo saw children dyed by chemical poisons. Elizabeth Butler saw girls with fingers that had been amputated at the knuckles by machines. And yet, these were not the only dangers working girls faced. Health inspectors and community social workers uncovered other silent killers that threatened not only the laborer but also the unsuspecting consumers.

The rag shop was in an old barn in Chicago. Its windows had been boarded over to keep thieves out. This also kept the dust in. When each new pile of rags was dumped on the floor, a cloud of dust rose. The rag pickers

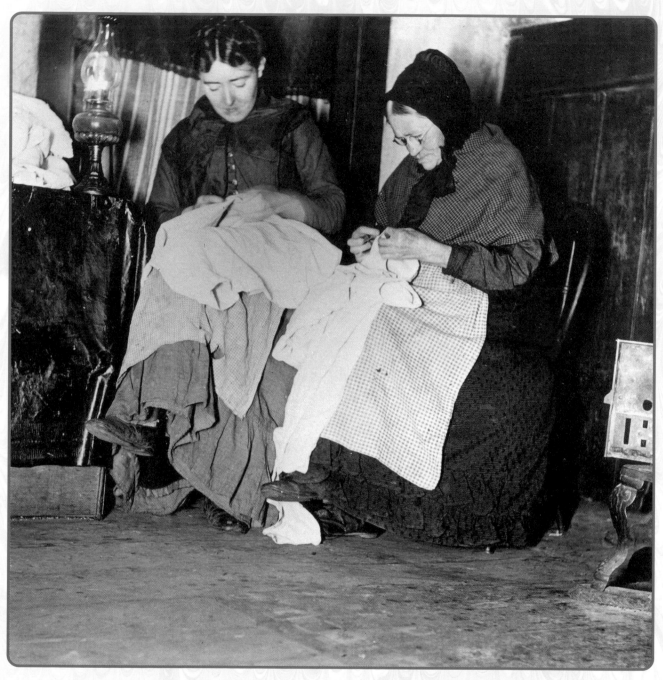

Originally published in Jacob Riis's book How the Other Half Lives, *this photo was titled "Sewing and Starving in an Elizabeth Street Attic."*

and rag sorters coughed and spit and the germs from their contaminated lungs mixed with the dust and settled on the rags again.

Contagious diseases like typhoid, scarlet fever, and tuberculosis spread quickly through the crowded, dirty tenements and sweatshops of Chicago, New York, and Pittsburgh. Workers—men, women, and children alike—sickened with the diseases continued to work nevertheless. Rosina, thirteen, worked all day long sewing linings and buttons on men's trousers. Her father and her older sister were lying in the same room, weakened with tuberculosis. They coughed and spat blood. When an investigator for a relief society discovered the sad situation, the society made arrangements to send the older sister to a hospital and to send Rosina to school. But the investigators could do nothing about the dozens and dozens of pairs of trousers that carried the tubercular infection and had already been delivered to the manufacturer for sale to the public.

The same story was repeated in hundreds of tenements. Maria Van Kleeck, who worked for a women's group called the National Consumers' League, met on one of her home visits a widow who earned a meager living sewing heavy cloth overcoats. Her son and three daughters sewed the coats, as well. A physician who examined the children found all were undernourished and weak. The boy, Angelo, was infected with scabies, a disease in which parasitic mites burrow under the skin. "The family owned only one bed," wrote Van Kleeck. For blankets, they used the very overcoats they were sewing. Of course, the mites had infected the fabric. "The physician recommended that all the clothing be burned and the rooms thoroughly cleaned," Van Kleeck reported. The landlord complied with the fumigation order, but also evicted the widow and her children.[19]

Inspectors could not tag and destroy all the contaminated clothing. Even if landlords or tenants fumigated their filthy rooms, disease was still rampant in the tenement districts and sickness returned. Widows and children still needed to work in order to live. A few months later, Van Kleeck discovered, the evicted widow and her sick children had found another room in another airless tenement and were sewing again.

"I bet you can't guess how old I am."
I look at her. Her face and throat are
wrinkled, her hands broad and scrawny;
she is tall. . . .
"Twenty," I hazard as a safe medium.
"Fourteen," she laughs.

BESSIE VAN VORST, THE WOMAN WHO TOILS [20]

At the end of a day, girls leave a Lynn,
Massachusetts, shoe factory

CHAPTER FIVE

Class Matters

"You'll never get away with it," friends told them. "Your hair, your speech, but especially your hands will give you away." Maria Van Vorst and her sister-in-law Bessie Van Vorst were ladies, not girls. They had been born into upper-class families and knew nothing of the grind of factory work. To have called them girls would have been an insult.

In Maria's home at Riverdale-on-Hudson, New York, a maid woke her in the morning. Other girls in her service—called domestics—prepared her meals, laundered her clothes, and scrubbed her floors. Maria wore Parisian clothes: a sealskin coat worth $200, a black cloth dress worth $150, and a silk underskirt worth $25. Working girls wore flannel and serge and coarse wool. Their shirtwaists cost $1.95; their woolen gloves, a quarter at most.

Maria dined on delicacies like truffles and *pâté de foie gras* (duck liver). The lips of ladies in her class were "reddened with Burgundies and cooled with iced champagnes." Not so the girls who worked for her. They ate beef stews and fried fish balls for breakfast.

Perhaps news exposés written by journalists like Nell Nelson who were called muckrakers or the findings of government investigations like the Reinhard Committee had spurred Maria and Bessie into action. Whatever the reason, the Van Vorst women concocted a daring scheme. They would give up all the finery of their class, abandon their comfortable homes along the Hudson River, put aside their sealskins and champagne flutes. They would assume new names and, with no friends to support them, each go separately in search of factory work.

They set out on their adventure—or perhaps more accurately their social experiment—in December 1901. Both women were idealistic but also naive. Neither was prepared for the blistering pain and fatigue of working for a living. Nor had they foreseen the humiliation they would face as Esther Kelly and Belle Ballard.

Esther Kelly

Bessie, who assumed the new name Esther Kelly, boarded a train for Pittsburgh. She wore plain clothes: a frayed hat, a flannel coat. Almost at once she felt a difference, not only in the way the clothes hung heavily and itched but also in the way others viewed her. She wrote:

I GET NO FARTHER THAN THE DEPOT WHEN I OBSERVE THAT I AM BEING TREATED AS THOUGH I WERE IGNORANT AND LACKING IN EXPERIENCE. AS A RULE THE GATEMAN SAYS A RESPECTFUL "TO THE RIGHT" OR "TO THE LEFT," AND TRUSTS TO HIS WELL-DRESSED HEARER'S INTELLIGENCE. . . . TO THE WORKING GIRL HE EXPLAINS AS FOLLOWS: "NOW YOU TAKE YOUR TICKET, DO YOU UNDERSTAND,

AND I'LL PICK UP YOUR MONEY FOR YOU; YOU DON'T NEED TO PAY
ANYTHING FOR YOUR FERRY—JUST PUT THOSE THREE CENTS BACK
IN YOUR POCKET-BOOK AND GO DOWN THERE TO WHERE THAT
GENTLEMAN IS STANDING AND HE'LL DIRECT YOU TO YOUR TRAIN."

Perhaps the gateman, eyeing Bessie's dress and her single bag, assumed her
to be a poor immigrant unfamiliar with the country and not knowing the
language. Bessie, however, understood only that her intelligence had been
insulted.

As the train approached the city, Bessie would have spied hillsides stripped
of trees and seamed with smokestacks, oil derricks, and cranes. She would
have passed mill buildings sided with sheets of metal. In the air above, like a
dark cloud, was smoke from the city's forty-seven iron and steel furnaces.
Bessie must have swallowed hard as she stepped from the train at noon, alone.
Her only connection to her former life was a purse pinned beneath her skirt.
Inside the silk bag was just enough money to pay her fare home.

The rivers were frozen black; the wind, icy. Along avenues webbed with
trolley rail lines, she began her search, first for a room to rent and second,
for a job. By dusk, she had found both. She felt encouraged. Her friends had
been wrong. No one had even asked her for her name.

The next morning, she reported for work
at a pickle factory. The superintendent sent her
to the top of a long flight of stairs. Here, when
the whistle sounded seven o'clock, she began
her first job: pressing cork liners inside tin jar-
tops. In the first three hours she fitted fifty
dozen caps. As in so much factory work, she was
simply another "hand," another cog in a machine
of working girls, some who emptied the bottles
and refilled them, some who corked,
labeled, and stamped the bottles, and some who
heaved and carried the full bottles away again.

*A trade card for the H. J. Heinz
Company from around 1900*

By ten-thirty, her shoulders had begun to ache. Her ears drummed from the machines. Her fingers stiffened and slowed. When she stopped to rest, a friendly voice beside her whispered a warning: "You'd better not stand there doin' nothin'. If *she* catches you she'll give it to you." *She* was the forelady, a girl no more than twenty years old. Bessie admitted to herself that she was afraid of her.

By the end of her first day, the hands that might have given Bessie Van Vorst away had blistered and bled. Already the transformation from a society lady to a working girl had begun. When she stepped outside the factory after her ten-hour shift, the night sky reflected the orange and red saw-toothed flames from the city's industrial furnaces. Pittsburgh was a city that worked all day and all night. For this day's work, Esther Kelly had earned a mere seventy cents.

By dawn, she was still so exhausted and muscle sore that she could not report for work. She did not show up again for work until Saturday. That day brought a new lesson in good girl work: Women, for no extra pay, scrubbed the factory floors after their Saturday shifts. Bessie wrote:

A PAIL OF HOT WATER, A DIRTY RAG AND A SCRUBBING-BRUSH ARE THRUST INTO MY HANDS. I TOUCH THEM GINGERLY. I GET A BROOM AND FOR SOME TIME MAKE SWEEPING A NECESSITY, BUT THE FOREWOMAN IS WATCHING ME. I AM AFRAID OF HER. THERE IS NO ESCAPE. I BEGIN TO SCRUB. MY HANDS GO INTO THE BROWN, SLIMY WATER AND COME OUT BROWN AND SLIMY. I SLOP THE SOAP-SUDS AROUND AND MOVE ON TO A FRESH PLACE. IT APPEARS THERE ARE A RIGHT AND A WRONG WAY OF SCRUBBING. THE FOREWOMAN IS AT MY SIDE.

"HAVE YOU EVER SCRUBBED BEFORE?" SHE ASKS SHARPLY. THIS IS HUMILIATING.

"YES," I ANSWER; "I HAVE SCRUBBED . . . OILCLOTH."

THE FOREWOMAN DROPS DOWN ON HER KNEES AND, WITH HER STRONG ARMS AND SHORT-THUMBED, BRUTAL HANDS, SHE SHOWS ME HOW TO SCRUB.

Belle Ballard

A week before Christmas, on a bitterly cold morning, Maria Van Vorst departed Boston by train and arrived in Lynn, Massachusetts. The shoe-manufacturing town had grown significantly from the days of Lucy Larcom and Sarah Trask. Now more than ten thousand operatives worked in the red-brick factories. Afraid of being homeless on a freezing night, Maria went first to the Young Women's Christian Association to ask for assistance. She told the woman there that her name was Belle Ballard. She was looking for work, she said, and needed a place to sleep. The older woman eyed the coarse woolen clothing. "A place in the shops?" she asked. Maria answered yes. The older woman then scribbled a name and an address on a piece of paper. "You must not go anywhere to sleep that you don't know about, child," she told her kindly. She offered to take her to her own home if the address on the piece of paper proved unsuccessful. It did not. Maria's room was the attic of a boardinghouse. The bed had no sheets, for which the landlady apologized.

"If any three things are more unendurable to me than others, they are noises, bad smells and close air," Maria Van Vorst wrote. Yet that was exactly the atmosphere of the Parsons shoe factory, where she went to work. The freight elevator door opened to a smoky room in which five hundred machines were roaring, tended by two hundred girls. Maria admitted that she was "green," and had never worked before. The forelady gave her a job as presser. Maria sat a table on which was an awl, a hammer, and a pot of glue. At once, the strong odor of the glue began to sicken her. All day, she painted glue on leather, turning down the gummed edges into seams, then hammering them in place.

Around her as she worked, the girls spoke of dances and boyfriends, of sick parents, of a mother who had died. Maria told nothing of her past. When a vendor walked through the factory with a basket of fruit and nuts, Maria bought an apple. It cost five cents. The girls around her seemed amazed at how easily she had spent the nickel. Although she had worked a few hours, Belle Ballard had earned just seven cents and here she was spending five. Maria cut the apple into pieces and shared it with them.

After a few weeks, Maria left Parsons to take a new job as a cleaner in Marches boot factory. Her job was to clean the caked glue from the leather boots, preparing them for sale. She worked on the sixth floor but no elevator took her to her work station. She climbed the stairs. Rags, some soaked in machine oil, and other debris cluttered the floor. The building had no fire escapes, though it was a state law. Through the grimy windows she could see only the rooftops of buildings. In case of a fire, the windows offered no hope of escape for her or the two hundred other girls.

She sat at a table with a crate full of boots nearby. Gone was the sickening glue pot. In its place was a glass of hot soapy water. Maria dipped her fingers into the glass and rubbed the soapy mixture over the leather to loosen the glue. After an hour's concentration, she paused to study the hands of her working girl neighbor. They were as leathery as the boots and stained nearly as dark. The nails of her fingers looked chewed. A dirty bandage wrapped one thumb. The woman noticed Maria's stare and explained.

"I LOST ONE NAIL; ROTTED OFF."

"HORRIBLE! HOW, PRAY?"

"THAT THERE WATER: IT'S POISON FROM THE SHOE-DYE."

SWIFTLY MY HANDS WERE CHANGING TO A FAINT LIKENESS OF MY COMPANION'S.

"DON'T TELL [THE FOREMAN]," SHE SAID, "THAT I TOLD YOU THAT. HE'LL BE MAD; HE'LL THINK I AM DISCOURAGING YOU. BUT YOU'LL LOSE YOUR FOREFINGER NAIL, ALL RIGHT!" THEN SHE GAVE A LITTLE LAUGH AS SHE TURNED HER BOOT AROUND TO POLISH IT.

Once she felt she had learned all she needed to know about pressing shoe leather and cleaning glue from boots, Maria left Lynn and her room in the cold attic. She was not yet ready to return to her former life. She intended to travel to Columbia, South Carolina, where she hoped to work for a time in a cotton mill. She boarded a train. In the dining car, she took a seat at a table and placed her order for a modest meal. She could afford nothing finer. Soon after, a group entered the car and sat. They wore furs and kid leather gloves. This was the class of people to which Maria Van Vorst belonged, but it was Belle Ballard now who was waiting, hungrily, for her meal. If they noticed Maria sitting nearby with her rough hands, stained now with blue indigo from the shoe dyes, they gave no sign. The porter, however, most certainly did. He served the better class of people first, Belle Ballard last. Maria would later write of the experience that angered her more than humiliated her:

> As I watched my companions in their furs and handsome attire eat, whilst I sat and waited, my woolen gloves folded in my lap, I wondered if any one of the favoured was as hungry, as famished as the presser from Parsons, the cleaner from Marches.

Thistledown and Fairy Hands

In Columbia, Maria found a room to rent from a Mr. Jones. She was not the only boarder in the house. The room—a loft above the kitchen without a door for privacy—was not hers alone, either. Nor was the bed. A mother ill with tuberculosis, her child, and another woman also slept in the small balcony over the kitchen. To reach the loft, Maria climbed a ladder.

She had taken a job as a spooler in the Excelsior cotton mill, one of the largest in the South. When the mill whistle sounded at four-thirty in the morning, Maria was already awake. The coughing of the mother in the bed and the sounds of the cook preparing breakfast below had stirred her from an uneasy sleep. The odor of fried food wafted to the rafters and hung in a bluish cloud above Maria's bed.

She ate her breakfast and joined the lines of other women, men, and children heading for the mill gates. She observed that those who labored inside all day had a distinctive hue to their skin—a sickly, sallow paleness. Once inside, Maria learned why.

The original caption of this 1910 photo taken in North Pownal, Vermont, reads: "Annie Laird, 12 years old. Spinner in a cotton mill. Girls in the mill say she is 10 years old."

The spinning spools gave off lint like a thousand dandelions gone to seed and blown by the wind. "Thistledownlike" was how Van Vorst described it. Around her, the workers constantly coughed and spat and cleared their throats, though the rumbling machines muffled the strangling sounds. Here was danger, Maria realized. Here were pneumonia and tuberculosis, the cause of the mother's deep coughs during the night.

Through the murkiness, she spied a little girl, standing on a box in order to reach the spindles. Maria described her:

> THROUGH THE FRAMES ON THE OTHER SIDE I CAN ONLY SEE HER FINGERS AS THEY CLUTCH AT THE SPINNING SPOOLS; HER HEAD IS NOT HIGH ENOUGH, EVEN WITH THE BOX, TO BE VISIBLE. HER HANDS ARE FAIRY HANDS, FINE-BONED, WELL-MADE, ONLY THEY ARE SO THIN AND DIRTY, AND NAILS—CLAWS: SHE WOULD DO WELL TO HAVE THEM CUT. A NAIL CAN BE TORN FROM THE FINGER—IS TORN FROM THE FINGER FREQUENTLY—BY THE FLYING SPOOLS. I GO OVER TO THE LITTLE GIRL.
>
> "HOW OLD ARE YOU?"
>
> "TEN."
>
> SHE LOOKS SIX. IT IS IMPOSSIBLE TO KNOW IF WHAT SHE SAYS IS TRUE.
>
> "TIRED?"
>
> SHE NODS, WITHOUT STOPPING.

Exhausted and dusted from head to foot with cotton fibers when the mill whistle sounded the end of the day, Maria trudged back to her rented room in the village. Most mill homes did not have a bathtub or indoor plumbing. In some mill villages, a public bathhouse was shared by all the residents. Certain hours and days of the week were reserved for men, for women, and for children. Yet even if Mr. Jones had had a tub and money to spare to heat hot water, Maria was too tired to have washed. She sponged her neck and arms with the basin of tepid water she had carried up the ladder to the loft.

When Maria Van Vorst returned to her home in New York, she began writing a novel called *Amanda of the Mill*. Although fiction, the character of Amanda was drawn, no doubt, from the girls with fairy fingers who worked the looms.

Brandied Cherries and Finger Bowls

With the experiment ended, Bessie and Maria Van Vorst returned to their former lives. What was the meaning of it all? their friends had asked. Bessie admitted that during the first three weeks she had viewed all working women as members of the same class of unfortunate people: slaves and miserable drudges, were her words. Once her muscles had toughened to the strain and her stomach had stopped cramping from the modest greasy food, she began to see the women as individuals. They fell in love. They had ambitions and dreams for their children. They were not a people to be pitied as she had once thought. Pity, in fact, had been a motivator for her part in the scheme.

The experience had changed Maria Van Vorst as well. The change of attitude was obvious one afternoon while she dined with a friend, a friend who owned one-half interest in a southern cotton mill. Maria described for her friend all that she had seen: the little girl with fairy hands, the mother so ill with tuberculosis that her coughing in the kitchen loft had kept Maria awake at nights, the little girls no higher than the spools they tended, the children asleep at lunchtime between the machines, too tired to even eat.

Her friend leaned forward to pick a brandied cherry from a dish. Maria watched her nibble it, then delicately dip her cherry-stained fingertips into a finger bowl on the table. Then her friend spoke. "Those little children—*love the mill!* They *like* to work. It's a great deal better for them to be employed than for them to run in the streets!"

Furthermore, the friend added, she needed the children to work in order for her factory to keep costs down and therefore remain competitive.

It was the same argument—work that was good for industry was also good for the girl. Maria Van Vorst no longer believed it. She had seen another side of that labor. In *The Woman Who Toils*, the book that she would one day write with her sister-in-law about their experiences, she wrote of the children:

> THEY FALL ASLEEP AT THE TABLES, ON THE STAIRS; THEY ARE
> CARRIED TO BED AND THERE LAID DOWN AS THEY ARE,
> UNWASHED, UNDRESSED; AND THE INANIMATE BUNDLES OF RAGS
> SO LIE UNTIL THE MILL SUMMONS THEM WITH ITS IMPERIOUS CRY
> BEFORE SUNRISE, WHILE THEY ARE STILL IN STUPID SLEEP.

What Maria did believe was that one day the little girls with fairy hands would rebel. They would grow into women who would raise their hands in fists above their heads and demand cleaner air and safer machines, shorter work days and wages enough to feed their own children.

Gurley Flynn called a meeting just for the women one day. She started with that lovely way of hers. She looked at us and said, "Would you like to have nice clothes?"
We replied, "Oh, yes."
"Would you like to have nice shoes?"
"Oh, yes," we shouted.
"Well, you can't have them. Your bosses' daughters have those things!"
We got mad. We knew it was true. We had shoes with holes, and they had lovely things.
Then she said, "Would you like to have soft hands like your bosses' daughters?"
And we got mad all over again.

IRMA LOMBARDI, PATERSON, NEW JERSEY [21]

The 1909 strike paved the way for other uprisings in which women played a part. In 1913 silk workers marched in New York City.

CHAPTER SIX

The Rebels

In the Eisendrath Glove Factory in Chicago, alarm clocks were ticking.

The management did not own the eighty-five-cent clocks. The working girls had each chipped in a nickel or as much as a dime to purchase them. Each morning they wound them up and set them where they could be seen from their work stations. Throughout the day the girls eyed the passing minutes, not wishing for lunchtime or suppertime but rather making certain that they were not falling behind in their piecework.

Every girl knows just how long it takes her to make any part of the glove, explained Agnes Nestor. *It is easy to lose a few minutes and not notice it until the end of the day when we count up our work and pay.*

Agnes never sewed a complete pair of gloves, just pieces of leather. She was paid by the piece. She took pride in her work and kept her eye on the ticking clock, earning three dollars a week. Overtime was mandatory, not a choice, and so Agnes packed two bagged lunches—one to eat at noon during the thirty-minute break; the other to eat at supper. On her first day of work, the rats that scurried across the factory floors had gnawed her supper bag, leaving her nothing. Agnes was fourteen and not much taller than five feet, but she was not a girl who was easily discouraged. In the days that followed, she outwitted the rats, hiding her supper in the sleeve of her coat.

Agnes Nestor

The girls frequently sang as they sewed. A favorite song was "A Bicycle Built for Two." The rhythm of the lyrics, Agnes found, kept her fingers working in time with the clock. One day the singing stopped, quite unexpectedly. The factory management had instigated a "speedup." They divided the work even more so that each operative would sew a smaller piece of the glove. The action meant increased production and profits for the company but decreased wages for the pieceworker. The girls had wound up their clocks each morning in an attempt to beat the piecework system. *It dimly dawned within us,* said Agnes, *that we were not beating the system. It was beating us.* The banders—girls who sewed only the bands on gloves— walked out first.

The girls in Agnes's department boldly spoke up. If the company tried to hire new girls to take the places of the banders, they told the foreman, then they would walk out, too. *We had taken a bold step,* said Agnes. *Almost with spontaneity we had acted in support of one another. Now we all felt tremulous, vulnerable, exposed.*

No one knew what might happen next. The girls had always resented the fees charged them for machine oil and needles. Now the fees seemed intolerable. Likewise, management rules that the girls had once accepted without much grumbling now seemed terribly unjust. Girls in one department could not eat lunch with girls from another department. The regulation isolated the workers, kept them from talking with one another and—more importantly—prevented them from uniting together against management.

A week later during lunch a group of girls in Agnes's department chipped in to buy a lemon cream pie. It was a feast they could scarcely afford. While sharing the sweet lemon dessert, the girls formulated a plan to strike for better working conditions. In her autobiography, Agnes described how the strike began.

> WE DECIDED IT WOULD BE COWARDLY TO WALK OUT AT NOON. WE WOULD WAIT UNTIL THE WHISTLE BLEW FOR US TO RESUME WORK, AND THEN, AS THE POWER STARTED UP ON THE MACHINES, WE WOULD BEGIN OUR EXODUS.
>
> SOMEHOW THE FOREMAN GOT WIND OF OUR PLAN. WE WERE FORMING A LINE WHEN REINFORCEMENTS FROM THE FOREMEN'S DIVISION SCATTERED AROUND THE ROOM, ORDERING US TO BACK TO OUR PLACES. WE BEGAN TO CHANT: "WE ARE NOT GOING TO PAY RENT FOR OUR MACHINES!" WE REPEATED IT OVER AND OVER, FOR THAT WAS OUR CHIEF GRIEVANCE.
>
> THE FOREMAN RETORTED: "THEY PAY FOR THEIR MACHINES IN THE EAST!"
>
> THAT WAS THE LAST STRAW. I SHOUTED BACK AT HIM: "WELL, WE ARE IN CHICAGO! WE DON'T CARE WHAT THEY DO IN THE EAST!"

The girls walked out. They could have taken the nearby stairs, but instead they walked through the adjoining rooms so that the girls in other departments who knew nothing of what was going on could see them leaving. Once in the street, Agnes took charge.

> I TOLD MY COMPANIONS THAT ALL WAS LOST UNLESS WE GOT THOSE OTHERS TO WALK OUT TOO. WE LINED UP ACROSS THE

The clocks had stopped ticking. The alarm had sounded.

Good Girls, Bad Girls

In Agnes Nestor's time, the late 1890s and early 1900s, worker rebellion was not new. Soon after the coming of machines, in the days of Lucy Larcom and Sarah Trask, both male and female workers had on occasion walked out of their jobs in protest for higher wages and against unfair factory regulations. In Paterson, New Jersey, in the summer of 1828, a new management rule delayed the lunch break by one hour. Angry child workers, "including a large number of girls," reported the New York *Evening Post*, walked out. During the same year in Dover, New Hampshire, more than three hundred girls turned out of the mill to protest a fine of twelve and a half cents for a minute's lateness. In 1836, mill girls who paraded through the streets of Lowell, Massachusetts, sang a mocking verse:

Oh! Isn't it a pity that such a pretty girl as I
Should be sent to the factory to pine away and die?

Such early resistances won little for the girls. Their failure was mostly due to their sex. Society viewed women as only temporary workers. Once they married, they were expected to leave the workforce. If they did not like their wages or workplace conditions, factory foremen told them, they could go elsewhere. Cheaper help, especially the growing number of immigrant girls, could—and did—replace them. Another factor against women's labor resistance was public opinion. Newspapers that covered strikes and turnouts in the mid-1800s reported little on the workers' grievances and instead focused on the good girls who had gone bad. A newspaper of the day, the *Boston Courier*, editorialized without sympathy during a strike: " . . . the girls ought to be thankful to be employed at all."

Women weren't the only workers walking off the job. Male laborers also wanted better wages, shorter work days, and safer working conditions. Some men formed secret organizations intent on terrorizing the owners into meeting their demands. The Molly Maguires was a band of Irish immigrant coal miners in Pennsylvania who set fire to company-owned buildings and dynamited railroad lines to disrupt the transportation of coal. Other men formed unions—such as the Metalworkers Union and the Meatpackers Union, for example—with the idea that by joining together as a single group laborers could force the owners of the factories and mills, railroads and coal mines to meet their demands. Many workers didn't trust union leaders or agree with union policies. They feared unions would become too powerful or that union-led strikes would do more harm to the worker than good. Even so, membership in labor organizations grew rapidly in the 1800s. The membership of the Noble Order of the Knights of Labor, begun in 1869 by a Philadelphia garment worker named Uriah Stephens, had within twenty years soared to 700,000 in cities across the country. The American Federation of Labor had 2 million members nationwide by 1914.

At first, women weren't invited to join these early unions for many of the same reasons that women's strikes had failed. Even union organizers believed that working girls were submissive and likely to leave a job once married. Women weren't fighters, and while most unions claimed to be peaceful, violence frequently exploded on the picket lines. And yet, some women did join unions. One of the first women to join the Knights of Labor was Leonora O'Reilly.

By the time that Agnes Nestor walked out of the Eisendrath Glove Factory, more and more women were attending union meetings and rallies, listening to fiery public speakers denounce the industry owners. Public opinion about unions was mixed. While some people sympathized with workers who were struggling to put food on the table, others believed union organizers were secretly plotting to overthrow the government. They called them anarchists.

As for striking girls, public opinion had changed very little from the days of Lucy Larcom. "A pack of wolves" was how one New York newspaper described a group of protesting women in 1902. Crowds of men, and some women too, heckled working girls who soapboxed—that is, gave speeches on street corners. "Go home and wash your dishes!" they cried. The good girl–bad girl stereotype remained strong. Rose Schneiderman's mother urged her not to strike and speak out, for then she'd never find a husband! Elizabeth Gurley Flynn separated from her husband, even though she was pregnant with their son, because he demanded she quit her union-organizing work and stay home with their children.

More often than not, the bad girls who walked out then cajoled their fellow workers to join them in the streets were the same good girls who had gone to work a few years earlier to help their families make ends meet. At thirteen, Rose Schneiderman took a job in a department store, then moved on to a capmaking shop. At sixteen, she was standing outside factory doors, urging women to come to union meetings. Pauline Newman, who as a child had been hidden from inspectors by her foreman under a pile of shirts in the Triangle factory, at sixteen led a tenement rent strike on the Lower East Side. Hannah O'Day began work at the age of eleven painting cans in a meat-packing plant in Chicago. A few years later, worn down by speedups, she tied a red silk handkerchief on the end of a stick and under this banner led the girls in her department out of the building and through the crowded, littered alleyways of Packingtown.

At fourteen, Agnes Nestor became the ringleader of the Eisendrath Glove Factory strike. The walkout ended a few days later without violence, and with little gain for the workers. Alice Henry, a journalist at the time who wrote for *Labor and Life*, blamed these strike failures on the girls' youth and inexperience. *The first step towards getting more wages,* said Alice Henry, *is to want more wages; to ask for more wages.* And yet, girls who got mad and simply walked away from their machines without a plan for fighting back and without support from the community—including money enough for food and rent to get them through days and weeks without wages—were doomed to fail, said Henry.

The Eisendrath walkout was Nestor's first strike, but it would not be her last. She was determined now to organize women into labor unions. She had learned an important first lesson in Chicago: A foreman will not miss a single girl, even a handful of girls. But should 1,000 girls walk out, or 4,000 girls or—even better—as many as 20,000 girls, *that* would surely silence the machines!

On a cold November night in New York City in 1909, it happened.

Picket Lines and Prisons

A common practice in most sewing factories in New York City in the early 1900s was for the forewoman to search her girls at the end of each day, making sure they had not tucked a bit of ribbon or thread inside their clothing. At sixteen, Clara Lemlich had bristled with humiliation whenever she was searched like a thief. A recent Jewish immigrant to the United States, Clara had begun work as a child in her native land, Russia. After just a few weeks in a factory in New York City, she began to rebel against hissing machines and abusive forewomen who allowed no time for her to think or speak. She attended union meetings. When she went on strike for better wages and shorter hours, her employer fired her. When she stood on soapboxes on street corners and spoke of workers' rights, hecklers splattered her with tomatoes. When she walked picket lines and refused to go home, the police beat her. By the time she was twenty-two, she had been arrested seventeen times.

In November 1909 labor activists had organized a mass meeting of shirt-waist workers inside Cooper Union in New York City. Clara Lemlich listened for hours, then asked to address the crowd. Many in the hall knew of her. *I am a working girl,* she told them from the speaker's platform, *one of those who are on strike against intolerable conditions.* She was tired of all the talking, she said. She was tired of people urging her to be patient until her grievances could be met. Then she called for a general strike and at once the women in their hats and long skirts jumped to their feet.

Above the shouts, Clara Lemlich asked for a commitment. *Will you take the old Jewish oath?* She raised her hand and said, *If I turn traitor to the cause I now pledge, may this hand wither and drop off at the wrist from this arm I now raise.*[23]

At once, two thousand hands went up. Two thousand voices repeated the vow.

Winter in New York City is cruel for a person without warm clothing, and without money to buy food or something hot to drink. Workers in shawls and thin-soled boots marched in picket lines through mud and ice. Two thousand soon became four, then five, then ten thousand as the strike spread from factory to factory throughout the city. The factory and sweatshop owners hired thugs and prostitutes to harass the strikers. Fistfights resulted in broken and bloody noses and bruised eyes and jaws.

Police, too, patrolled the picket lines. They shoved the strikers, then clubbed them when they refused to disperse. They arrested the strikers on numerous charges—most often disorderly conduct, but also assault. They dragged the girls bodily into wagons and brought them to court where a judge, more often than not, took the word of the police officers over that of the strikers. By the end of December, more than seven hundred women had been arrested. Nineteen had been sentenced to a women's insane asylum on Blackwell's Island in the East River where, in coarse striped prison uniforms, they served their jail time scrubbing floors.

The strike spread beyond New York City as still more women joined the rebellion. In Chicago, Agnes Nestor was deeply involved in the strike. More than ten years had passed since her first experience at Eisendrath. In that time she had grown into a formidable labor leader, a powerful speaker for workers' rights at rallies not just in her home city but in cities in the East. During the strike, she went to Philadelphia to establish a headquarters where striking women on the picket lines could come for hot coffee and soup. She also appeared in court each morning with money from the union organization to pay bails for girls who had been arrested the night before. The bails were five and ten dollars, an incredible sum for a worker who had been without wages for weeks. If an arrested striker could not pay the fee, the judge ordered her locked in jail for days. Much of the bailout money came from society ladies, women in the same class as Bessie and Maria Van Vorst, who supported the strikers' cause. The society ladies helped in other ways, as Agnes described in her autobiography.

SINCE MANY OF THE GIRLS WERE BEING CHARGED WITH ACTS NOT COMMITTED, WE DECIDED TO HAVE AS OBSERVERS PARTICULARLY WELL-KNOWN WOMEN OF PHILADELPHIA WHO WOULD FIND OUT AT FIRST-HAND WHAT WAS REALLY HAPPENING IN THE PICKET LINE AND WHOSE WORD WOULD BE TAKEN IN THE COURTS.

MISS FRANCES TRAVERIS COCHRAN, THE DAUGHTER OF ONE OF THE OLD AND WEALTHY FAMILIES OF PHILADELPHIA, CAME INTO OUR STRIKE HEADQUARTERS ONE AFTERNOON TO SAY THAT SHE WANTED TO GO OUT WITH ONE OF THE PICKETS AS AN OBSERVER. THAT EVENING ONE OF THE STRIKERS CAME AND TOLD ME THAT FRANCES COCHRAN HAD BEEN ARRESTED. AS EVERYONE KNEW THE YOUNG LADY'S REPUTATION AND STATUS IN THE CITY, HER ARREST MADE QUITE A STIR.

Miss Cochran was not a "girl." She was a lady. Once the police sergeant realized his mistake, he apologized and released her at once. To the sergeant's surprise, she refused to go. Miss Cochran, at least, saw no difference between a working girl and a lady on the picket line.

"WE WERE BOTH DOING THE SAME THING," SAID MISS COCHRAN. "WE WERE WALKING UP AND DOWN THE STREET. THEREFORE WE BOTH SHOULD BE TREATED ALIKE."

Both were released. In New York City, however, Martha Gruening was not forgiven for her devious behavior. The daughter of a well-known physician, she walked the picket line in clothing that did not reveal her social status. Police arrested her with another girl. Agnes Nestor described what happened the next morning when the magistrate realized Gruening's true identity.

WHEN MISS GRUENING, BROUGHT BEFORE THE MAGISTRATE THE NEXT MORNING, GAVE HER NAME AND BACKGROUND AND DECLARED SHE WAS NOT A STRIKER, THE MAGISTRATE WAS FURIOUS.

"I WAS AT THE FACTORY ONLY TO SEE IF ARRESTS WERE MADE UNJUSTLY," REPLIED MISS GRUENING.

THIS MADE THE MAGISTRATE MORE INDIGNANT THAN BEFORE.

"I CHARGE YOU WITH INCITING A RIOT AND HOLD YOU FOR FIVE HUNDRED DOLLARS BAIL!" HE DECLARED.

THEN HE CHARGED: "IT IS THE WOMEN OF YOUR CLASS, NOT THE ACTUAL STRIKERS, WHO HAVE STIRRED UP ALL THIS STRIFE. HAD YOUR KIND KEPT OUT OF THIS FIGHT, IT WOULD HAVE BEEN OVER LONG AGO!"[24]

In the magistrate's eyes, Martha Gruening had sunk to the low level of a common working girl. He fined the girl who had been arrested with her two hundred dollars, a fortune that she could never pay.

The strike continued through January. Labor organizers like Agnes Nestor, Rose Schneiderman, and Pauline Newman traveled around the country seeking more donations of food to feed the strikers and their families. In Buffalo, New York, Pauline Newman spoke to wealthy women's groups during the day. *The strikers were starving,* she told the wealthy women. Court fines alone had already topped one million dollars. Newman raised thousands of dollars for the cause. *And then I moved on,* she said, *to Rochester, then Syracuse.*

On February 15, the union ended the strike. Some factories had come to an agreement with their workers. Others did not. In some shops, gains had been made. But other concerns, in particular safety concerns, had been put aside in favor of other benefits—a shorter work week of fifty-four hours, for example. Some managements—the Triangle Shirtwaist Company in New York was one—promised to correct all safety and sanitary violations if only the girls would return. The management's words sounded reassuring, and the girls were weary. They went back.

The strike became known as the rising of the 20,000, though as many as 40,000 girls—most of them twenty-two years and younger—may have walked off their jobs. Despite its uneven gains, the uprising changed good girl work forever. Instead of getting angry and walking out with no plan, the girls had begun to band together. They joined unions in greater numbers than ever before. They had the growing support of the community, including a sisterhood with society ladies like Martha Gruening. The girls had nicknamed these ladies of class "the mink brigade" and some working girls, including Leonora O'Reilly, distrusted them. Yet without their support during the rising of the 20,000, many more girls would have gone to jail.

Perhaps most important, however, was the change in attitude of the girls themselves. The first step in getting better wages, Alice Henry had said, was to want better wages. The girls had shown their fellow male workers—and the world—that they could fight. In a rally in New York City during the strike, twenty women who had been arrested sat before the speakers' platform. Each wore a white sash. The word "arrested" was printed on some; "workhouse prisoner" was printed on others. If they were considered bad girls for striking for their rights, then they were prepared to accept this label. A reporter for the *New York Call* captured this attitude in a single line: *"Jail has no terror for girls who have been confined for years in workshops that are worse than a prison."*[25]

The workers had broken the stereotype that for so many years had been a yoke of submission around their necks.

*This is not the first time girls have been burned alive
in the city. Every week I must learn of the untimely
death of one of my sister workers . . .*

ROSE SCHNEIDERMAN

*The Triangle Shirtwaist Company was located on the top three
floors of the Asch Building in New York City. On March 25, 1911,
a fire began that would be the last straw for working women
fighting for fair treatment and safe conditions.*

CHAPTER SEVEN

Broken Promises, Vows Renewed

Three generations of women in Leonora O'Reilly's family had worked in factories. Her immigrant grandmother, upon arriving as a widow in the United States in the 1840s, had kept her family from starving by sewing. Leonora's mother, Winifred O'Reilly, had carried baby Nora in a laundry basket to work at Seligman's. Leonora herself had quit school early to add her cents a day to the family income.

There came a period in Nora's life, a friend confided, when Nora had become very bitter and saw only ugliness in the working world around her. "All the sweetness, all the sunlight seemed to have gone out of her heart," the friend wrote in a letter. "Often would I hear: 'Pigs, pigs, all of them!'"

O'Reilly broke through her despair. She met with other women workers to discuss the meaning of life beyond machines and to talk of more practical, immediate matters: how to organize, how to improve their lives. She also recaptured a dream and returned to school. She wrote to a friend in 1898:

> . . . FROM EIGHT O'CLOCK IN THE MORNING UNTIL SIX O'CLOCK IN THE EVENING, I AM THE SERVANT OF GEO. E. BELLAMY; THAT IS, I SERVE HIM AS FOREWOMAN IN HIS SHIRT FACTORY, FOR WHICH I RECEIVE ENOUGH MONEY TO KEEP BODY AND SOUL TOGETHER, TO BUY ENOUGH STATIONERY TO WRITE TO YOU, AND A FEW OTHER FRIENDS, TO PAY MY DUES IN ONE, TWO, OR THREE CLUBS; AND NOT A CENT FOR A RAINY DAY!

Winifred Rooney O'Reilly and Leonora O'Reilly

At night, however, Leonora lived a different life. She entered a world that had been closed to her years ago when she was forced to leave school as a girl. It was a world of art and literature and philosophy, and it freed her. *Rules stiffen the mind* she jotted in the margin of her diary. In the same letter to her friend, she wrote:

> I AM STUDYING EVERY NIGHT IN THE HOPE OF MAKING SOMETHING MORE OF MY LIFE THAN A MERE MANAGER TO MAKE MONEY FOR SOMEONE ELSE TO SPEND.[26]

In 1900, Leonora earned her normal school degree. She quit the factory and devoted herself to the newly formed Women's Trade Union League. Through the league and its Manhattan Trade School she taught other working girls vocations so that they could acquire skills and with their skills demand higher wages, better jobs, and better lives.

O'Reilly's convictions—as well as those of thousands of girls who had vowed to improve working conditions for women—were put to a severe test late on a Saturday afternoon, March 25, 1911. The fire in the Triangle Shirt-waist Company in New York City began with an explosion. Flames spread quickly through the eighth and ninth floors of the building, trapping hundreds of working girls. The panic that followed could only be imagined in the mass of burned bodies found huddled against the factory doors afterward. Terrified girls jumped from the windows, some with their arms wrapped around one another. The force of their fall tore through the fire nets and the blankets held by firefighters in the streets. William Shepherd, a reporter who witnessed the horror, wrote, "The flood of water from the firemen's hoses that ran in the gutter was actually red with blood."

Of the 500 workers—mostly women and girls—146 had died, either burned to death or broken on the pavement when they had jumped. The dead were carried down the flights of stairs, one body at a time, and taken to a nearby pier where the city opened a temporary morgue. The bodies were so badly burned that many would not be positively identified for weeks.

DOORS WERE LOCKED SAY RESCUED GIRLS, reported *The New York Times* two days after the fire. Quoted as its source was Leonora O'Reilly. *I have just come from a luncheon we prepared for the unfortunate girls who escaped,* the reporter quoted O'Reilly. *They all told me one thing—that the doors were locked. Eighteen of our workers have been going the rounds of the families of those having employment. In every family they tell the same story.*

The practice of locking doors, she explained, was to keep latecomers out and to prevent the girls already inside from walking out in a mass protest. It was the same in other factories throughout the city, she said. *I assure you it is,* she stated emphatically. In fact, locked doors had been a specific grievance during the rising of the 20,000 two years earlier, the newspaper now reported. Then, weary of the long strike, Mr. Blanck of the Triangle Shirtwaist Company had promised the Women's Trade Union League that all safety violations would be speedily corrected.

"We thought he had seen the justice of our demands for decent working conditions," said Mary Drier, the president of the Women's Trade Union League. "We trusted him, and allowed our girls to go back."

The impact of the Triangle Shirtwaist Company fire was felt around the country, as these newspaper cartoons suggest.

The fire haunted those who had worked so tirelessly for working girls' rights—Pauline Newman, Clara Lemlich, Agnes Nestor, Leonora O'Reilly. All their speeches and their strikes had been in vain, at least for those 146 girls who had died. A bitterly angry and grieving Rose Schneiderman addressed the members of the mink brigade during a memorial service for the victims of the fire. *I can't talk fellowship to you who are gathered here. Too much blood has been spilled. I know from experience it is up to the working people to save themselves.*

You really gave them hell, Pauline Newman told Rose afterward.[27]

What else could the working girls do but continue the struggle?

Leonora O'Reilly had been there in Cooper Union on the night Clara Lemlich raised her hand and vowed not to turn traitor to the cause. Despite the horror of the fire, or perhaps because of it, Leonora O'Reilly and others like her renewed their vows.

Two days after the fire, speaking on behalf of the Women's Trade Union League, Leonora O'Reilly proposed the formation of a new committee that would guard as secret any information a working girl brought to it. *The New York Times* carried the questions that would hopefully identify other fire-traps in the city:

ARE THE DOORS LOCKED WHILE YOU WORK?
ARE THERE BARS ON THE WINDOWS?
ARE THERE FIRE ESCAPES ON ALL FLOORS?
ARE THE ESCAPES READILY ACCESSIBLE?
ARE SCRAPS OR WASTE ALLOWED TO ACCUMULATE
NEAR THE MOTORS OR STEAM PLANT?

IF SO, YOU WORK IN A FIRE TRAP. YOU MAY SECRETLY DESCRIBE
YOUR CONDITION BY CALLING AT THE HOMES OR WRITING TO MRS.
STEPHEN WISE, 23 WEST 120TH STREET; LEONORA O'REILLY, 680
SEVENTH AVENUE; MRS. BEARD . . .

The fight for justice for working girls had begun anew.

Thirty Days
in the Tombs

The demands for decent wages and hours for working girls did not end when the shirtwaist strikers returned to their factories in February 1909, nor were they met in the public outcry following the Triangle Shirtwaist Company fire in 1911. The struggle would continue for many years more and at times, would be every bit as brutal and bloody as the rising of the 20,000.

Margaret Hinchey had worked as a forewoman in a laundry service. A year after the fire, during a strike against unhealthy conditions and long hours, she, too, walked out with her girls. Her employer blacklisted her. On the picket line, a policeman arrested her for assault though she had struck no one. In court, a judge sentenced her to thirty days in the city jail of New York, a grim place known as "the Tombs."

She went willingly, unafraid, knowing that she had been sentenced out of malice. Her own behavior in fighting for her rights had been admirable, she believed, and that made her prison sentence tolerable. Yet, seeing strikers in the same cells with prostitutes—as if, she said, there were no difference between them—saddened her. There were young girls who had stolen ribbon from the factory. There were madams, women who ran houses where girls sold their bodies in another desperate way to earn a living. She described them and herself standing at the bars "like so many monkeys, looking out into the corridor."

The "mean things" of prison life during her thirty days bothered her: *The coffee-pot so rusty inside that the stuff boiled in it tastes like medicine, pallets so narrow that they're scarcely wide enough for your shoulders and you can't turn in them, spoons thick with the rust on them.*

But the image of good girls and bad girls standing together at the bars of their cells, young girls and women too old to work in factories, yet forced to scrub the concrete prison floors—*that* seemed most unjust. *What kind of a country is it,* she wondered, *that builds prisons for its grandmothers?* [28]

The image did not defeat her, however. Nor did the blacklisting, the sentencing, or thirty days in the Tombs. It made her stronger. The struggle was far from over. In fact, it had only begun. More strikes, more bloodshed, and more deaths were in the future for good girls who worked. Margaret Hinchey was ready for the fight. She would not be alone.

Use me in any way you can for the good of the cause, she told Leonora O'Reilly of the Women's Trade Union League. *I am yours to the end.*

NOTES

1. Agnes Nestor, *Woman's Labor Leader: Autobiography of Agnes Nestor* (Rockford, IL: Bellevue, 1954), pp. 4-5.

2. Patricia Cleary, "She Will Be in the Shop: Women's Sphere of Trade in Eighteenth-Century Philadelphia and New York," *The Pennsylvania Magazine of History and Biography*, July 1995.

3. *Colonial Records of North Carolina and Annals of Southwest Virginia, 1769-1800* as quoted in Julia Cherry Spruill, *Women's Life and Work in the Southern Colonies* (New York: Norton, 1972), p. 58.

4. Quoted in Mary H. Blewitt, *We Will Rise in Our Might: Workingwomen's Voices From Nineteenth-Century New England* (Ithaca, NY: Cornell University Press, 1991), pp. 60-61.

5. Ibid., pp. 61-62.

6. Quoted in Benita Eisler, ed., *The Lowell Offering: Writings by New England Mill Women* (Philadelphia: Lippincott, 1977), pp. 46, 52-53, 56-57.

7. "Portrait of a Franco-American Grandmother," WPA Life Histories Federal Writers' Project Collection, Library of Congress.

8. Jacob A. Riis, *How the Other Half Lives* (New York: Dover, 1971), p. 38.

9. "East Durham Mill Village," WPA Life Histories Federal Writers' Project Collection, Library of Congress.

10. Quoted in Sarah Atherton, *Survey of Wage-Earning Girls Below Sixteen Years of Age in Wilkes-Barre, Pennsylvania* (New York: National Child Labor Committee, 1915), pp. 9, 29-30, 31.

11. "National Biscuit Company Workers," WPA Life Histories Federal Writers' Project Collection, Library of Congress.

12. "Lucille Hicks," WPA Life Histories Federal Writers' Project Collection, Library of Congress.

13. Nell Nelson, *White Slave Girls of Chicago* (Chicago: Barkley, 1888), p. 39.

14. Ibid., pp. 62-63.

15. The collected papers of Mary K. O'Sullivan, Schlesinger Library, Radcliffe College.

16. Quoted in Grace Abbot, *The Child and the State, Volume I* (Chicago: University of Chicago Press, 1938), pp. 425-426.

17. Quoted in Philip Foner, *Mother Jones Speaks: Collected Speeches and Writings* (New York: Monad Press, 1983), p. 453.

18. John Spargo, *The Bitter Cry of the Children* (Chicago: Quadrangle Books, 1968, reprint of the 1906 Macmillan edition), p. 171.

19. Maria Van Kleeck, "Child Labor in New York City Tenements," *Charities and the Commons*, January 18, 1908.

20. Quotes in this chapter are from *The Woman Who Toils* by Mrs. John and Maria Van Vorst (New York: Doubleday, Page & Co., 1903).

21. Quoted in Stewart Bird, Dan Georgakas, and Deborah Shaffer, *Solidarity Forever: An Oral History of the Industrial Workers of the World* (Chicago: Lake View Press, 1985). Copyright 1985 by Stewart Bird, Dan Georgakas, and Deborah Shaffer.

22. Nestor, pp. 30-31.

23. Lemlich's oath is quoted in Barbara Mayer Wertheimer, *We Were There: The Story of Working Women in America* (New York: Pantheon Books, 1977), and in Philip Foner, *Women and the American Labor Movement: From Colonial Times to the Eve of World War I* (New York: Routledge, 1990).

24. Nestor, pp. 109-110.

25. Quoted in Theresa Malkiel, *The Diary of a Shirtwaist Striker* (Ithaca, NY: Cornell University Press, 1990, reprint of the 1910 edition copyrighted by Theresa Malkiel), p. 31.

26. From the collected papers of Leonora O'Reilly, Schlesinger Library, Radcliffe College.

27. Quoted in Annelise Orleck, *Common Sense and a Little Fire: Women and Working-Class Politics in the United States, 1900-1965* (Chapel Hill: University of North Carolina Press, 1995), p. 66.

28. Hinchey's story was found in the O'Reilly papers, Schlesinger Library, Radcliffe College.

INDEX